A GALAXY OF GOVERNESSES

A GALAXY OF
GOVERNESSES

Bea Howe

GALAXY: Noun, a brilliant and beautiful
assemblage: a group of English ladies
(*From a Victorian Dictionary*)

DEREK VERSCHOYLE
THIRTEEN PARK PLACE, ST JAMES'S, LONDON SW1

First published in 1954 by
Derek Verschoyle Limited,
13 Park Place, St James's,
London, SW1

Made and Printed in Great Britain
by Adlard & Son Limited,
The Bartholomew Press, Dorking

To Mark

CONTENTS

LIST OF ILLUSTRATIONS

PROLOGUE

Though the life of the English Girl has been fully dealt with in such well-documented books as *English Girlhood at School* by Miss Dorothy Gardiner and Miss Dorothy Stuart's *The Girl Through the Ages*, little about the family governess, who stood at her side, giving her her first lessons and teaching her to behave as a lady should, has been recorded.

From what background did she come and how did she find her way into the family? Where did she first give her lessons and what clothes did she wear? How much money did she earn? These were some of the questions which I found myself asking and which set me to try and write the story of the English family governess.

I soon discovered that many top-ranking governesses, who achieved fame apart from their governess-life, like the three Brontë sisters, Mrs Elizabeth Elstob, the Saxon Lady, and Mary Wollstonecraft, have had their 'governess phase' treated perfunctorily by their biographers. For this reason the professional journals of Miss Weeton in Regency times and later Miss Emmeline Lott and Mrs Maria Graham are valuable records of their calling. However poorly trained at first and amateurish in her efforts at teaching young girls, the family governess held an unrivalled position for observing domestic English life with its ever-changing social customs and class snobberies. If more of her observations had been preserved, they would have been of definite interest to students of social history.

My approach to my subject is a personal one and influenced largely by the material that turned up during several years of arduous research. For only now and then in some unpublished journal kept by an affectionate pupil like little Grace Sherrington in the reign of Queen Elizabeth, did my heroine, the Governess, leap suddenly into life. How delightful it was, then, to meet charming Mistress Hamblyn making her sedate way across the lawn at Laycock Abbey, or later to come across vulgar little Miss Elphick in Elizabeth Grant's *Memoirs of a Highland Lady* when, 'with hair a-crop and a leg fit for a buskin', she made such a hit as Rosalind in a school-room version of *As You Like It*, staged by the Grant family at Rothiemurchus in Regency days.

My chief trouble was that so many intriguing governess-portraits like Jane Austen's Miss Sharpe who taught the Knight children at Godmersham, or Lady Anne Lindsay's Hennie the Sylph at Balcarres were mere sketches, too faintly drawn for one to try and complete them.

For the governesses that I have tried to feature as being most representative of their period, there are many others whose story will never be written. I leave their dim ghosts still haunting the school-rooms of long ago. Against the background, though, of her professional life, the Governess, that poor gentlewoman, alternatively bullied and baited or loved and appreciated for close on four centuries, emerges, I think, as a very gallant figure. When opportunity did happen to knock on the door of her school-room, she nearly always rose from her chair and answered the call, particularly when the summons came for her to go abroad. The most formidable people are those who take the rightness of their beliefs so much for granted that it never occurs to them to question it. During the nineteenth century, the English governess reigned supreme in the continental school-room and brooked no interference by the very placidity of her conviction that the English manner of doing things was the only one conceivable.

There was not a corner of the globe to which she did not go, bearing with her our traditional way of life, secure in her loyal hands for the benefit, not only of her pupils, but for mankind in general.

Over the considerable length of time that I took to assemble the material for this book, I have been helped in many ways by many kind friends and acquaintances. It would be difficult to acknowledge all such help but I should like to thank in particular: Miss Champernowne for the use of family papers and important records she had already collected on Katherine Ashley, and Lord Hastings for permission to reproduce her portrait by Clouet Janet; the late Duke of Devonshire for access to the Trimmer Letters (1786–1829) kept at Chatsworth and Mr Francis Thompson, MA, FSA, Keeper of the Collections and Librarian, for his kind help and advice over my chapter on Selina Trimmer; Miss Florence Green, Librarian of Brentford and Chiswick Libraries, for producing the picture of the Trimmer Villa in Windmill Lane, Brentford, after much search; Lady Cecilie Goff for remembering the Tablet to the much-loved Governess at Great Durnford Church, near Salisbury, and Mrs Baird for copying it out so kindly; Mrs J. Varley, MA, County Archivist for Lincoln, for confirmation of various details concerning Catherine Swynford's later life and death at Lincoln; Miss Nancy Mitford and Messrs Chapman and Hall for their kind permission to quote from *The Ladies of Alderly*; Lady Mander (R. Glynn Grylls) for allowing me to draw on material in her book, *Claire Clairmont* (John Murray); the Brontë Society, Haworth, for permission to reproduce the prospectus; the late Mrs Gotch for invaluable assistance which led to the discovery of the unpublished journal kept by Maria Graham, and Mr Gastão Nothman, late attaché for Cultural Relations at the Brazilian Embassy, for permission to quote from the manuscript; Doña Victoria Ocampo for details regarding her governess Miss Ellis; the late Miss Edith Davidson for the story of her governess experiences in two World Wars, and Mrs Henry Studholme for being our means of contact; Fitzroy Maclean, MP, for allowing me to expand his own sketch of Mary Fellows in *Eastern Approaches*; Messrs Arthur Barker for permission to quote from *Siamese Harem Life* which they reprinted, and Mrs Anna Leonowens Monahan of Montreal for her immediate response to a last-minute appeal for a portrait of her grandmother, Mrs Anna

Leonowens; Mr Beattie, CA, Secretary of the Governess Benevolent Institution, Victoria Street, London, for material and use of books in the GBI Library; Miss Vera Douie, Librarian of the Women's Service Library for her sympathetic help in matters of research and for producing always the necessary book; the British Museum for the pictures of Bathusa Makin, Elizabeth Elstob and Richmal Mangnall; the Victoria and Albert Museum for Redgrave's 'The Poor Teacher'; and the National Portrait Gallery for Lawrence's portrait of Maria Graham. Lastly, I wish to thank Sylvia Townsend Warner and my husband Mark Lubbock, for their support and encouragement, without which I might have attempted but certainly not finished my book.

CHAPTER ONE

First Origins of the Governess

GOVERNESS! What long hours of boredom this word evokes! Hours of enforced confinement in a drab schoolroom; of endless dos and don'ts; of the sharp tap of a ruler on wood; of blackboards and smudgy exercise books; of dreary afternoon walks taken in London parks or through country lanes; of light-weight suppers consisting of a glass of milk and *petit beurre* biscuits on a tray; even of perpetual correction. It depended on whether one had the mediocre kind of governess determined to have a good time and with an eye open to the main chance, like Becky Sharp, 'who did not pester young brains with too much learning but, on the contrary let them have their own way in regard to educating themselves,' or the severe authoritative type, another stern Miss Fennimore, who thought it an insult to be offered a pupil below her teens or to lose one till nearly beyond them.

But who was the first professional governess? From what country did she hail? During the nineteenth century, England held the monopoly for the supply of the best nannies and governesses to the world in general. They formed part of our top-grade exports. A wonderful fifth column planted into the most exclusive foreign nurseries and schoolrooms, they wielded immense though secret powers of influence. For no parent, however loving, can undermine the influence of the hand that rocks the cradle or guides the first quavering pothook to success.

Did we produce the first governess? No, the first mention of this super-heroine in unremunerative drudgery comes in the letters of St Jerome to the Christian ladies of his circle – to a certain Roman lady, the Lady Laeta, whose little daughter,

Paula, had been vowed to the religious life from birth. St Jerome was much concerned over the education of this child. As soon as Paula began to push her stilus laboriously over a wax tablet, he advised that an elderly hand should be put in charge of her unsteady fingers, and take control of her infant mind. In fact, she was to have a governess. She was not to be a pretty girl either. She was to be a melancholy dame. An 'honest woman of sad age'. A governess : *gravis, pallens, sordidata, subtristis*. These are St Jerome's own words. So the portrait of a governess was first drawn in sombre black and white by a saintly man of God.

Consistently through the ages, though there were many exceptions, of course, the governess whom Charlotte Brontë described as having 'the pale despondent looks of her class' has been the most popular and ever-recurring type.

After all, it was not so very difficult for the first governesses in England to conform to St Jerome's portrait, for the little learning there was, was centred in the religious life. Those grave, quiet women of stately name like Hildelith, Abbess of Barking or Eadburga of Minster might be said to have been our first amateur governesses. Courageously, they carried the flickering torch of learning for women through dark and difficult times. Their schoolroom was the nunnery; their pupils either pious nuns being trained to take their place or those early Saxon princesses called by queer, outlandish names like Heresuid, Sethrid, and Ethelburga, who were taught by the holy women to spell and write, to read the Holy Fathers and to compose Latin verse as well as to spin and embroider.

Towards the eighth century, court education began to impinge on the scholastic province of the nunnery and girls of royal and noble birth stayed at home for instruction. Thus the palace-school of mediaeval times came into being. Charlemagne established a famous one at his palace of Aachen about 789 which served as a working model for others on the continent. But it was not until King Alfred started his great labour of reviving education in Dane-ravaged

England, that we could boast of a recognised palace-school of our own. Once one was established the sons and daughters of Eadward the Elder, Alfred's son, were carefully trained at it. In this palace-school, we catch a fleeting glimpse of a very early royal governess (she might well have been the first), who bore the dignified name of Elfgifu. But we shall never know whether Elfgifu conformed, or not, to St Jerome's ideal of a pale, sad teacher.

After the Norman Conquest, a fresh element from abroad was introduced into the palace-schools. This was the new gospel of chivalry, 'the discovery that life could be built upon love, that every knight and every lady must love and the highest glory of a man was to own the domination of a lady!'

Born in Provence, of leisure hours in a warm climate, the 'gay saber', as the new creed was called, was alien to England. It took time for our grave Saxon princesses and countrified ladies, convent-bred, to acquire the fashionable Norman-French way of deportment, together with courtly turns of speech. Women had to give pleasure now to the opposite sex by sweet singing and graceful dancing. They had to learn how to entertain and be witty. The art of polite conversation was introduced and more elegant table-manners. Those heroines of romance that move so easily through the French *lais* and *chansons de geste* of this period are the true denizens of that exquisite tapestry-world one associates with the Châteaux of the Loire. A world where Time seems to be perpetually fixed at spring. Escorted by milk-white hinds or the fabulous unicorn of heraldry, these tiny childish figures, apple-breasted and supple as a willow-wand, embroider only, or sing to the lute. How could the sombre governess ordained by good St Jerome participate in the training of such ethereal, faery figures?

For a brief interlude, then, as brief as spring itself, our melancholy dame of learning undergoes a complete metamorphosis. Chameleon-like, she changes her whole nature and we find her second portrait in verse; the supple, vivid verse of a great English poet. She is even re-named by him. For

17

that prim and solemn word 'governess', Chaucer substituted his own gay term 'maistresse!' Thus newly-christened, the mediaeval governess takes up her stand beside the slim Blanchfleures and Blondes, the gallant Johannes and Eleanours of Plantagenet England. She does not give her pupils a book of prayers to read or the Holy Bible like the devout Saxon Abbesses. Instead, she hands them a skein of crimson silk with which to embroider some quaint heraldic beast on a cushion; she teaches them to play some curiously-shaped musical instrument. She is their careful guide and friend as well as being their duenna. A woman of the world, disillusioned and a little weary, who might have sinned herself, and repented, she is all the better equipped to guard young innocence from her own experience. Schooled in all gracious arts of how to entertain and jest with men, the mediaeval governess or 'maistresse' helped to spread the gospel of the 'gay saber' over England.

This type of wordly education for 'lordes doghtres' found its natural home in the castle-bower rather than in the secluded shade of convent walls. In *The Phisicien's Tale*, Chaucer addressed those ladies responsible for a girl's upbringing thus:

> ' And ye mistresses in your olde lyf,
> That lordes doghtres han in governaunce,
> Ne taketh of my wordes no displesaunce,
> Thenketh that ye ben set in governinges
> Of lordes doghtres, only two thinges ;
> Outher for ye han kept your honestee,
> Or elles ye han falle in freletee,
> And knowen wel y-nough the olde daunce
> And han forsaken fully swich meschaunce
> For evermo ; therfore, for Cristes sake,
> To teche hem vertu loke that ye ne slake . . .
> Of alle tresons sovereyn pestilence
> Is whan a wight bitrayseth innocence.'

When Geoffrey Chaucer wrote these lines did he have in mind one of the most successful governesses of all times? She was his sister-in-law, the beautiful Catherine Swynford, born in 1350, who was the youngest daughter of Sir Paon Roelt, Guyenne King of Arms. A Knight of Hainault, he had come to England in the service of the enlightened Queen Philippa, Queen to Edward III.

Catherine had the good fortune to be sent as a young girl into the household of the well-educated Duchess Blanche of Lancaster, a charming woman, much loved by her husband, John of Gaunt, brother of the King. In 1368, Catherine married Sir Hugh Swynford of Kettlethorpe in Lincoln, one of the Duke's gentlemen-at-arms, and when the good Duchess Blanche died while her husband and Sir Hugh were abroad, fighting, Catherine was appointed governess to the Ladies Philippa and Elizabeth of Lancaster, her daughters.

It was about now that the children of the reigning house in England came to have a state, or lady, governess appointed to control their households, usually separated from their parents. As this position carried great responsibility and influence, the leading noblemen of the day would scheme to have a female member of their families chosen for the post. Chief qualifications of the lady governess were wisdom, tact and a thorough knowledge of court customs then in fashion; in rank, she was usually an earl's or baron's wife. These hand-picked ladies, as one might say, controlled the royal children's household, seeing that they were well-dressed, well-fed, and well-educated by tutors who were well-known clerics. The lady governess usually named the sub-governesses under her; they had to be skilled embroideresses as fine needlework came high up in the list of a mediaeval princess's accomplishments. In Plantagenct times, much elaborate work was done at court in gold and silver thread. As French was the court language till almost the end of the fourteenth century, all royal governesses and their pupils had to be bi-lingual.

But Dame Catherine Swynford was far more than 'only the governess' to the Ladies Philippa and Elizabeth. She was virtually their guardian during the absence of their royal father, territorially the most ambitious man in England. It has been recorded that John of Gaunt's daughters were among the first ladies who learned to write in mediaeval England. This speaks well for Catherine's supervision. For a woman to write at this time was as rare as it was for her to possess a library, however small, of illuminated books and missals. Naturally, with her Hainault ancestry, Catherine could speak good French.

In 1371, John of Gaunt returned home with his second wife, Constance, only daughter and heiress of Don Pedro the Cruel, the deposed King of Castile. Their marriage had not been a love-match, merely one of political convenience; through his wife, Gaunt hoped to acquire Castile, one day.

Sir Hugh Swynford did not return home with his master, and it was soon rumoured that His Grace of Lancaster was constantly paying 'visits to the nursery', not so much to see his daughters, as to talk to their young, accomplished governess. He had declared himself very much satisfied 'with the good and agreeable service our very dear and beloved Dame Catherine Swynford has done for our beloved daughters Philippa and Elizabeth.'

The Middle Ages had set up rigid standards of beauty to which all ladies of fashion conformed. Their hair had to be of a gilt-like fairness and their eyes of an odd bluish-grey colour known as vair. Figures were supple-boned and thin, in order to carry off the long, tight-fitting gowns, trimmed with fur at the hem, which Queen Philippa had introduced from the Continent and over whose bodices a tight spencer, or *cote-hardie*, was often worn.

Catherine Swynford was, no doubt, a natural blonde with eyes of vair. In the 'nursery', then, at the Castle of Leicester, the Duke's favourite home, she would sit with a piece of needlework held in her 'longe fingres smale'. Her hair was glossily coiled inside a gold fret, or caul, that covered her tiny shell-like ears – a hair-style brought in by Queen Philippa. They must have made a handsome pair; the slender golden-haired governess and the royal Duke, a tall spare man, as a portrait shows him, with a small yellow forked beard. Even as their liaison began, Sir Hugh Swynford had the tact to die abroad. By 1372, Dame Catherine was recognised everywhere as the Duke's official mistress and a child was born.

In the years that followed several more children appeared who took the name of Beaufort or 'Faerborn' as the wags of Richard II's court called them. By this time, old King Edward III had died and John of Gaunt, the most powerful figure in England, was acting as Regent for his young nephew Richard. On account of his high position, perhaps, Gaunt suddenly broke off his rather questionable relationship with Catherine Swynford, and tongues ceased wagging over the private life of his most puissant Grace of Lancaster.

Quietly, Catherine removed her children to the household of Mary de Bohun, wife of Harry of Hereford, her lover's eldest son. Catherine appears to have been on excellent terms always with her quasi step-children and her presence in the Lancaster family circle was never in the least resented. During her long and strange career, she never put a foot wrong and was the essence of tact which, after all, is the most useful trait for any royal governess to possess. So she remained biding her time while she brought up her clever Beaufort children, and administered her estates in Lincoln and Nottingham.

Unpopular both with the English common people and the young 'intellectuals' now in power at court, John of Gaunt went abroad when he gave up the Regency. His father-in-law had died and he wished to acquire Castile in the name of his second wife, Constance.

On her death in 1394, his way was made clear. Barely two years later Dame Catherine Swynford, his ex-mistress, walked majestically up the great nave of Lincoln Cathedral to marry, in all pomp and pageantry, her royal lover at the High Altar. Court circles were again shocked and gossip rife. But in spite of many cold looks and malicious whispers, Catherine appeared before her nephew-in-law, King Richard, and took her place as third Duchess of Lancaster with dignity.

Catherine brought nothing to her ambitious husband but brains and beauty. She had neither a rich English duchy to offer him like his first wife, Blanche, nor a foreign kingdom like Spanish Constance. But when a marriage was arranged between Richard II and Princess Isabella of France, it was Catherine, who, as the King's senior aunt, went to Calais to escort the child princess to England.

A year later, her three Beaufort children were solemnly made legitimate by a special Act of Parliament. She had won even this delicate round.

On the death of her husband, 'time-honoured Lancaster', Catherine retired to Lincoln where she inhabited a house belonging to the Dean and Chapter. John of Gaunt had been a considerable benefactor to the Cathedral, presenting jewels, vestments and hangings devised by himself.

In Lincoln, Catherine spent the rest of her days salving her conscience probably by doing good works. She died in the extreme odour of sanctity on 10th May 1403 and was buried in a large tomb under a stone canopy carved with a design of marguerites, near the High Altar of the Cathedral. Her daughter lies in a smaller tomb beside her.

Catherine's is the earliest 'success story' of what a clever governess, blessed with brains and beauty achieved in such a remote time as Plantagenet England.

From the brilliant Beaufort family which Catherine Swynford founded, there emerged finally three sucessive Kings of England. First, there was Edward IV, her great grandson, through the marriage of her grand-daughter, Cicely Nevil, the Rose of Raby, to Richard, Duke of York. Secondly, Richard III, brother to King Edward IV. Thirdly, came the scholarly Henry Tudor, crowned King Henry VII, who was the son of her great grand-daughter, the learned Lady Margaret Beaufort, Countess of Richmond. So it can be said that Catherine Swynford was the governess-ancestress of a race of Plantagenet and Tudor Kings remarkable for their intellectual and artistic gifts. Her unique achievement has never been equalled.

After the Black Death had swept through England like a mighty curse, there was such a flight of foreign teachers to the Continent for safety, that Anglo-French (till now the reigning courtly language) disappeared as a medium of instruction in the grammar schools. All England welcomed the revival of the old mother-tongue, English. A period of social distress followed and with such subtle influences at work as the Peasant's Revolt and the Dissolution of the Monasteries, a completely new system of education for girls came into being.

Among the 'gentle' classes, typified by the smaller landed gentry, a daughter's early lessons in needlework and manners came to be given by her mother or a resident lady governess (if her parents could afford one), while a smattering of French, music and dancing were acquired from visiting male tutors. After this preliminary training, a young girl was provided with her own 'duenna' and sent to a household superior to her own. Here, under the direct care and tutelage of its mistress, she stayed till a suitable husband was found for her. If marriage was not her lot, she became 'waiting-woman' to her mistress or even 'gentle-woman' in the service of some really high-born dame. The peak of this particular form of career was an ultimate appointment at court as maid-in-waiting to the Queen herself. This system of female education, known as 'placing-out' or 'advancement', peculiar to England, gradually led to the establishment of proper boarding-schools.

So influential powers of teaching came to be vested directly in the housewife. This was the day of the stately homes of England; of busy bustling households, run by efficient Paston and Percy ladies. The castle-bower was no more and many of the big religious houses closed, never to re-open. *How the Good Wiff taughte her Doghter*, which appeared in 1420, describes, through its title, how solid British housewives were playing their part in preference to the gay 'maistresses' of Chaucer's day. In the 'Good Wiff's' book, emphasis is laid on the art of running a house, of seemly female behaviour, of regular church-attendance, of wifely submission and tact in dealing with a difficult spouse. These precepts may all sound rather middle-class and sober contrasted to the romantic surveillance and wordly experience of the maistresse. But England was growing rich and stable through the steady rise to power of her own sturdy middle class. So the sensible and sane advice of the 'Good Wiff' is thoroughly in keeping with the spirit of the times. With the establishment, too, of England's influential Trade Guilds, backed by thriving family life, a firm basis was being laid for the coming 'professional' woman, from whose ranks would eventually step the first salaried teachers and governesses.

Towards the end of the fifteenth century, the whole outlook of women's education becomes more hopeful. Slowly but surely there developed an intellectual freedom which was to release women from their age-old routine of embroidering and singing, of dancing and spinning, and from generally being considered charming dolls engaged in entertaining the opposite sex on the one hand or sober, solid housewives in fustian on the other. This complete change of outlook was entirely due to the Renaissance. Great scholars and thinkers like Erasmus, Vives, Thomas Becon (the Reformer) and Edward Mulcaster regarded the Renaissance woman more as a 'rational being' and 'man's desired companion' than as a charming doll or prosaic housekeeper.

Thus a fashion for learning, a love of the classics and the study of Latin, French and Italian, started in such high places as King Henry VIII's court and at Lord Dorset's country-house, Bradgate, where small, serious Lady Jane Grey was kept ever close to her books by her ambitious parents. They wished her to outdo in study, her clever royal cousins, the Ladies Mary and Elizabeth Tudor.

This cult also spread to simpler homes, like Sir Thomas More's Chelsea Manor, where his charming daughters were being educated in the new Renaissance spirit.

With such examples to follow, Tudor girlhood was spurred on to receive the classical education given to their brothers.

In those comfortable new manor houses, being built every-where, in rooms with lattice windows and oriels instead of narrow loop-holes, sisters studied the ancient tongues, read heavy theological books, played sweetly on the clavichord and virginals. They sang the ayres of John Dowland or Thomas Nashe and the Early Lutenists; learnt the secrets of pestle and mortar in their mother's still-room; and memorised well-tried family receipts against the time when marriage re-moved them far away from maternal supervision. They were taught to read and embroider skilfully by faithful and fond governesses like Mrs Katherine Ashley, who was appointed governess to Princess Elizabeth in 1536 and never left her through all the vicissitudes of her long life, either as perse-cuted princess or triumphant Virgin Queen. Queen Elizabeth has been quoted as saying 'she brynketh me up from the cradell to the throne'.

Mrs Ashley

Katherine Ashley was the daughter of Sir Philip Champer-nowne of Modbury, Devon, whose family was of Norman des-cent. Her eldest brother, John, was said to have been a favourite of King Henry VIII's because of his 'quaint conceits'. Her second brother, Sir Arthur Champernowne was Vice-Admiral of the West who served Queen Elizabeth gallantly at sea.

In 1536, when the Princess Elizabeth was about three and beginning to learn her letters from 'a delicate little horn-book of silver filagree', Katherine Champernowne was appointed to be her governess. She had been warmly recommended for this important post by Thomas Cromwell. For nine years Katherine Champernowne controlled her household, not an easy task as her royal pupil's star was in sad eclipse through the execution of her mother, Anne Boleyn, and the birth of her delicate little half-brother, Prince Edward.

In 1545, Katherine married John Astley, second son of Sir

Thomas Astley of Norfolk, and a first cousin of the ill-fated Anne Boleyn in whose train he went to court. In olden days, a surname was often spelt in a variety of ways even in the same letter or legal document. Thus Katherine spelt her name Aschyly (and is known in history as Ashley) though when Roger Ascham, a friend of her husband's, wrote to her, he spelt it correctly. 'Gentle Mrs Astley, would God my wit wist what words would express the thanks you have deserved, for that noble imp your labour and wisdom now flourishing in all goodly godliness, the fruit whereof doth even now redound to her Grace's high honour and profit.'

He expresses his love for her husband and stresses her own gentle kindness to William Grindall then alive and himself. He concluded his letter with this sound advice: 'If you pour much drink at once into a goblet, the most part will dash out and run over; if you pour it softly, you may fill it even to the top, and so her Grace, I doubt not, by little and little may be increased in learning.'

I find this letter of Ascham's very interesting in the light of all the plays, novels and biographies which have recently appeared on the great Queen Elizabeth and her times. For they depict Katherine as a stupid chattering gossip, in character far more like a nanny than a royal governess. Would a man of Roger Ascham's brilliant intellect and acumen have wasted his time or words on a trivial-minded woman? I doubt it.

There is Katherine Ashley's portrait, too, reproduced for the first time here. It shows the face of an attractive and alert young woman with an amused expression and dark, full, liquid eyes. She is sombrely but richly dressed as denotes her high post. Beside her is a painted skull which is supposed to symbolise humility. Again, I ask, would Elizabeth, even as a young girl, have tolerated a silly creature about her to control her household and teach her those things that only one woman can another?

When King Henry VIII died in 1547, his widow (Katherine Parr) married the Lord High Admiral, Sir Thomas Seymour, uncle to the frail boy-king Edward VI, and brother of the Protector Somerset. Princess Elizabeth, rising fifteen, precocious and vital, went to live with her stepmother the Queen Dowager and her new husband in Chelsea. And there, all the trouble began for Mrs Ashley. Very soon after the Princess's arrival she caught the handsome Admiral, then nearing forty but a fine, dashing figure of a man, coming into her Royal pupil's bedroom, to play with her and tease her, familiarly. His foolish behaviour is fully detailed in Katherine's confessions which are kept at the Records Office, signed Kateryn (or Katheryn) Aschyly.

Katherine did all she could to stop Seymour's unseemly behaviour. Although he swore he meant no harm, she went finally to the Queen Dowager and reported to her on the giddy romping that went on in the Princess's bed-chamber. The Queen Dowager was as much perturbed as the governess. She ordered Mistress Ashley to take her royal charge to Cheshunt while she bore off her fond but foolish husband to Sudeley Castle in the Cotswolds, there to wait with her for the coming of their child. Two days after its birth, Queen Katherine was dead.

Katherine Ashley made a grievous mistake now which was to cost her pupil and herself dear. Although she had taken such exception to the Admiral's behaviour as a married man, as a widower, she advised her young pupil to write him a letter of condolence. But Elizabeth had learnt her lesson. 'I will not do it, he needs it not', she is recorded to have told her governess. 'Then,' replied Mrs Ashley, 'if Your Grace will not, then will I.' This she proceeded to do. What was in her head at this time and why did she write?

It must be remembered, I think, that young King Edward's frail life hung by a thread. Should he die, England was faced by a fanatical Roman Catholic revival on the accession of Princess Mary, the next heir to the Throne. Katherine Ashley was a good churchwoman, always in fear that death or imprisonment might overtake her beloved pupil. Perhaps she thought it might be safer for her after all to marry the Lord High Admiral, a brave Englishman and a staunch Protestant to whom the country looked in preference to his cold, calculating brother, the Protector. Life at Cheshunt was probably dull and, to enliven the daily round, everyone in the household began to talk of what might or might not be the Lord High Admiral's future marriage plans. Lady Tyrwhit, ex-lady-in-waiting of the Queen Dowager, went so far as to repeat that 'it was the opinion of many that the Lord High Admiral kept the late Queen's maidens together for the Lady Elizabeth whom he intended to marry shortly'.

Aloof and lonely in this world of secret, back-stairs gossip stood the grave figure of the fifteen-year-old Lady Elizabeth, in the velvet cap and sober Tudor dress which she effected at the time to draw as little attention to herself as possible. She said nothing. She wrote nothing. But in spite of her discretion disaster overtook both herself and her governess.

A fortnight before Christmas, Mistress Ashley was sent for from Hatfield and told by the Duchess of Somerset, the Protector's wife, that 'she was not worthy to have the governance of a King's daughter'. Almost immediately afterwards she was arrested with Thomas Parry, the Princess's Treasurer and imprisoned in the Tower where Seymour also lay, accused of high treason against the State and his brother the Protector Somerset.

A confession was soon wrung from the quaking Parry, followed by another from the royal governess. While defending herself, Katherine Ashley begged forgiveness 'for this my gret foly yt wold ether talke or spoke of maryage to such a personage as she ys'. Then she prayed that her prison cell might be changed 'for by my trothe yt ys so cowlid yt I cannot slepe yn hyt and so darke yn the daye or I stope the wendo with straw thar ys no glass'.

During this time, it was February by now, Elizabeth was constantly interviewed and questioned by the King's Council. But never once did she lose courage or her head. Finally, she sat down and wrote in her beautiful script one of the most brilliant and subtle letters ever penned by a woman, defend-her good name and her governess's.

'I am the bolder to speak for another thing; the other was because peradventure your Lordship and the Council will think that I favour her evil doing whom I shall speak for, which is for Katheryn Ashley, that it will please your Grace and the Council to do good unto her. Which thing I do not favour her in any evil (for that I would be sorry to do) but for these considerations which follow . . . First because she hath been a long time with me, and many years, and hath taken great labour, and pain in bringing me up in learning and honesty – therefore I ought of my duty to speak for her, for Saint Gregory sayeth that we are more bound to them that bring us up well, than to our parents, for our parents do that which is natural to them, that is, bringeth us into the world, but our bringers up are a cause to make us live well in it . . .'

Never before or since has a royal governess been lodged in the Tower on a charge of high treason; never before or since has a princess championed her cause as Elizabeth Tudor championed the cause of Katherine Ashley, her governess. She knew that she owed her dear single-hearted Ashley years of devoted service. She knew that she had erred only out of love and fear for her future. Elizabeth was far more bound by her affection to her governess (as she herself had admitted) than to any parent. What had her father, the late King, ever done for her or her poor feckless mother? Elizabeth concluded her letter to Somerset, begging him to be lenient too 'to Master Ashley, her husband, which because he is my kinsman I would be glad should be well'.

All was well eventually. Well for the governess, the hus-band, and the treasurer. For they were all three released from the Tower and after a discreet interval of time had elapsed they re-joined their royal mistress at Hatfield.

In 1553 came the Wyatt Rebellion when Princess Elizabeth

was put in the Tower and for a while Katherine was placed in the charge of Sir Roger Chomeley. The following year, they were together again. But 1556 saw Mrs Ashley once more lodged in the Tower on account of the Dudley Plot which was to marry Elizabeth to Courteney and dethrone Queen Mary and Philip. Katherine denied all knowledge of this and was released along with the Princess's three maids of honour, who had been taken with her. Her husband had by this time escaped abroad to be free of religious persecution.

When Elizabeth came to the Throne in 1558, Mistress Ashley was reinstated with full honours in her service. She was made Chief Lady of the Bedchamber and her husband, John Astley, Master of the Jewel House. A year later, the intimacy of the Queen with Robert Dudley roused much speculation and many thought that Mrs Ashley was privately urging the Queen to marry Leicester. On the contrary, from the Hapsburg papers, it has come to light that the Chief Lady of the Bedchamber had fallen at Her Majesty's feet, one day, and implored her in God's name to marry nobly and put an end to the current disreputable rumours. Elizabeth was told by her old ex-governess that her behaviour with her Master of the Horse occasioned much evil gossip and her subjects would in time become discontented. Then there would be bloodshed, for which she would have to give account to God : 'rather than this should happen,' continued Katherine, 'she would have strangled Her Majesty in the cradle.' They were strong words to which Elizabeth replied that she well knew these were the outpourings of a good heart and true fidelity; that she was quite willing to marry in order to console her and all her subjects but that she had no wish to change her state, and such a marriage must be well weighed.

The marriage in question was to Archduke Charles and was being pressed by the Imperial Ambassador at Court. Elizabeth never married the Archduke Charles, Leicester or any other man, and to the end of her life, her ex-governess knew much of what was concerning Her Grace's mind. But she never betrayed that confidence. In Her Majesty's Bed-chamber at Greenwich Palace or Nonsuch she kept faithful guard and waged, no doubt, her own private war against the ravages of time and the moth upon that fantastic collection of heraldic gowns, bejewelled stomachers and feathered hats in her care.

On the 18th June 1565, Katherine Ashley died still in the service of her beloved pupil. She died, not in the odour of sanctity like Catherine Swynford, but in the musty sweetness of musk, cloves, and pomander balls that clung to the velvet hangings and curtains of a great Queen's bedroom. That same day, the Spanish Ambassador wrote to his master, Philip II: 'On the 18th Mistress Ashley, the Queen's governess died. Her Majesty went to see her the day before, and I am told she is greatly grieved . . . '

So the Queen mourned her faithful Ashley and refused to grant audience on the day of her death. The court mourned too, the passing of a sympathetic personality. For a year later Hugh Fitzwilliam corresponding with Her Majesty said: 'Now that Mrs Ashley is gone he has no friend to take his moan to.' The present head of the Astley family is Lord Hastings, amongst whose heirlooms is a beautiful wallet of soft leather worked in silver filagree, with silver mountings engraved with a Crucifixion and Wolsey's name, which was left to Katherine by the great Cardinal and Churchman. This significant gift, coupled with the deep abiding affection of a great Queen, belies the rôle of a silly old woman that poor Katherine Ashley has been made to play so long.

During the middle of the sixteenth century, Thomas Becon, the Reformer, began to agitate for the still better education of women. For the first time, he puts into concrete form the plea that grammar schools for girls should be formed. 'It is expedient', he writes, 'that by public authority schools for women children be erected and set up in every Christian commonweal, and honest, sage, wise, discreet, sober, grave, and learned matrons made rulers and mistresses of the same, and that liberal stipends be appointed for the said school-mistresses which shall travail in the bringing up of young maids, that by this means they may be occasioned the more gladly and willing to take pains.'

We are back at the portrait drawn by St Jerome of his ideal governess: that sad and sombre lady who was to instruct little Paula. In his description, the Reformer omits only the adjective *pale*. But Becon made this great contribution: the resigned figure, destined to sit discreetly and gravely in the future schoolrooms of England, was to have professional status and a stipend.

From where was this body of female teachers and gover-nesses to be recruited? As a class, they were virtually non-existent.

Still, the scene had been set for the possible entrance of a fully qualified woman teacher. In 1562, Edward Mulcaster, an enlightened schoolmaster, seconds Becon's plea for women's schooling to be set on even broader lines. His writ-ings voiced the growing sense of public obligation; that concept of 'civil and domestic duty' so characteristic of the Elizabethan era.

'Is not a gentlewoman', he sums up, 'thoroughly well-equipped who can read distinctly, write neatly and swiftly, sing sweetly, draw well, understand and speak the learned languages, as well as the modern tongue approved by her time and country, and who has some knowledge of logic and rhetoric besides the information acquired in her studies of foreign languages? If in addition to all this she be an honest woman and a good housewife would she not be worth wishing for and worth enshrining?'

There is nothing here that the humble family governess cannot aspire to, for here are allied the graceful accomplish-ments of the chivalrous age with the sensible and sound axioms of the 'Good Wiff'. Here, too, the golden light of a summer's afternoon, is suddenly focused on the oriel win-dow of a country house in quiet Wiltshire in the year 1562.

Katherine Ashley

Forma nihil, si Pulchra perit; sed fectoris alma
Divini species, non moritura viget
W. M. sculpsit

Bathsua Makin, a portrait by Marshall

Below this window sits a child whose name is Grace Sherrington. She is co-heiress with her two younger sisters of her father, Sir Henry Sherrington of Laycock Abbey. Beside her is Mistress Hamblyn, her much-loved and much-honoured governess, dressed in a simple stuff gown. She has a strong sweet face and I hazard that her Christian name might have been Margaret. Earnestly the two heads, the child's soft fair one and Mistress Hamblyn's coifed by a spotless white kerchief, are bent over a vast book. It is Doctor Turner's excellent *Herball*, much read by little Grace's governess. Outside, the lovely lawns of Laycock lie green and smooth. The rooks are cawing familiarly in the ancient elms and a sweet scent of lavender, thyme, and bergamot drifts in through the window from the knot-garden outside. Here, in the typical surrounddings of an old and beautiful country-house, that still survives today, we find our first genuine salaried English governess.

Mistress Hamblyn

The charming figure of Mistress Hamblyn provides the best example of the poor but loved relation (she was orphanniece to Sir Henry Sherrington) who undertook the education of her young cousins. But, unlike many of her contemporaries, Mistress Hamblyn received a proper salary for her duties.

At the exhibition of private ancient documents in Lincoln's Inn Great Hall during the Festival of Britain was a letter of Sir Philip Sidney's. In it, he asked his Steward Walker to give his sister's 'olde governess Mrs Anne Mantell the summe of twentie powndes which is dew unto her for wages'.

This letter dated 1576 places Mrs Mantell as a contemporary of Mistress Hamblyn and tells us what the salary might be of a Tudor governess. Mistress Hamblyn was highly honoured by the Sherringtons and we are repeatedly told that her wise counsel was always sweetly given. She must have had a way with children, for little Grace Sherrington so de-

C

lighted in her company that she wrote years later: 'I would sit with her all dae in her chamber and by my goodwill would never goe from her, embracing allwaies her rebukes and reproofs.'

At Laycock with its enormous staff of indoor and outdoor servants, gossip and tale-bearing was rife. It was a wise woman like Mistress Hamblyn, who not only knew but kept her place so tactfully. From the first, she stressed to little Grace Sherrington the importance 'to deal truly and faithfully in all things, both in small matters and in greate, to beware of all lyes and oathes and reporting of newes; to hear much and speak little, seeming to be ignorant in some things rather than to boast of knowledge that we have not and thereby give occasion to be laughed att'.

Mistress Hamblyn was not a blue-stocking in the classic sense. In her simple country schoolroom she taught the young Sherrington girls, 'to cypher with the pen, to cast up and prove great sums and accompts, to write letters and read'. She also taught Grace to sing psalms and to do needlework. Her favourite teaching manual appears to have been Doctor Turner's *Herball*. Learning for aristocratic young women was fashionable as Queen Elizabeth who could make impromptu speeches in Latin, French and Italian was on the throne. But in quiet Wiltshire, Grace Sherrington did not learn Latin and Greek, but rather how to run a large establishment and staff; to be a good letter-writer; and a fine herbalist. When, at the early age of fifteen, she married young Anthony Mildmay and went to live at the Mildmay seat in the Midlands she took away with her pious habits of devotion and domestic interests that belonged to country home-life rather than to fashionable society. During the long years of her married life she was always able to amuse herself at home. Her husband, Sir Anthony, was much away and she spent a great deal of time alone. Then she could 'spend tyme in works of myne owne invention, without sample or pattern or carpets or cushion worke, and to drawe flowers and fruitt to their life with my plumett upon paper. All of which varietie did greatly recreate my mind.'

She never forgot her governess and draws a vivid portrait of her in her private journal. 'She proved very wyse, religious and chaste, all good virtues that might be in a woman very constantly settled in her, for from her youth she made good use of all things that ever she did see or hear and observed all companys that ever she came into, good or bad, so that she could give a right censure and sure judgement of most things and give wise counsell upon many occasions. . . . She had also good knowledge in phisick and surgerie. She was of excellent quicke spiritt and plesently conceited; her mirth was very savoury and full of wit and in her sadness she uttered forth nothing but wisdom and gravatie.'

Lady Mildmay adds this warning postcript: 'If all fathers and mothers were so careful and provident and governesses put in trust were so diligent and faithful as mine, their off-spring would not be so wicked and unfortunate.'

Though these charming words were written a long time ago, they still illuminate the portrait of that kind and gentle Tudor governess, Mistress Hamblyn, who maintained in her wise and simple teaching the best traditions of an English gentlewoman.

Laycock Abbey remains one of our first country houses; a show place, unique, unspoilt, now the property of the nation. It is a pleasing thought that beside this golden-grey pile of Bath stone, where once the learned monks taught, the ghost of one of the most honoured members of her race may still walk. Mistress Hamblyn might so easily have been a despised relation; another Cinderella, ignored in her schoolroom. Instead she was much loved and appreciated, which the Victorian family governess rarely was, even though she lived in a, supposedly, more enlightened era.

CHAPTER TWO

The Seventeenth Century Governess

'They who undertake the difficult Employ of being an Instructress or Governess of Children should be persons of no mean birth or breeding, civil in deportment, of an extraordinary winning and pleasing conversation.'

MRS HANNAH WOOLLEY, *The Gentlewoman's Companion* (1675)

Queen Elizabeth died in 1603 and with her the golden age of learning for women which her remarkable gifts of scholarship had inspired. Although there was a growing demand for women teachers and good family governesses after the pattern of Mistress Hamblyn, social conditions necessary to supply that demand were adverse. Young women who wished to teach girls, professionally, met with strong opposition and criticism. Only a minority group of writers like Thomas Becon, the Reformer, supported the theory of having a nucleus of properly paid and trained governesses. Everyone else believed that a woman's place was in the home and if she must teach, it was not to be Latin or French but an odd hotch-potch of so-called feminine accomplishments like straw-work, bugle-work, wax-work and japanning, for which only a meagre salary was obtained. Consequently, there were many well-bred girls who could not read or write properly during the first half of the seventeenth century. These girls, when orphaned, were forced to enter some large country-house for their sole means of livelihood. They did not become governesses like Mistress Hamblyn but 'waiting' or 'tiring' women, usually, to my lady. As Miss Gladys Scott-Thomson has pointed out in her book, *The Russells in Bloomsbury*, these gentlewomen held a special position in English country-houses which corresponded to that of 'squire' or 'page' on the men's side. Their names did not appear, for instance, on the household salary list. At a suitable time many of them married the family chaplain, or local parson, and set up their own establishments, bringing what culture of the 'big' house they had assimilated to village life.

At the outbreak of the Civil War in England, family life was completely disrupted and well-bred girls were educated as best they could be while their Cavalier and Roundhead fathers fought one another, and their mothers, valiant women often like Lady Bankes of Corfe Castle in Dorset, defended their homes and children with a mere handful of loyal servants against the enemy. Conditions for education must have been similar in many ways to those we have experienced recently when our war-time schoolrooms were set up in queer remote places out of reach of air-raids, flying bombs, or threat of invasion, with scratch equipment and lessons conducted at any odd time. Naturally, serious learning could not flourish. Aping French fashions introduced at court by Queen Henrietta Maria, Cavalier girls spent too much time over their clothes, on dancing and reading frothy romances. So said pious Roundhead mothers intent on a sober home-training for their daughters which involved serious study of the Bible and lessons in good housewifery.

When Cromwell was made Protector, children became solemn little creatures, who addressed their parents as 'Sir' and 'Madam' and stood gravely bare-headed in their presence. The rod was rarely out of their teacher's hand and lessons began early – at the age of three or four – in the Commonwealth schoolroom.

About this time a young orphan set out to be a governess. She was barely seventeen and could play and dance a little. She knew 'the smooth Italian indifferently' but could instruct on all the elegant period arts like 'Beugle-work upon Wyres' and 'Cutting of Prints'. Shrewd and sensible with a kind heart, and a nice sense of humour, Hannah Woolley was shocked to see how harshly children were treated. As an older woman, happily married, with thirty years of teaching experience behind her, she sat down and wrote *The Gentlewoman's Companion* which first appeared in 1675. In it, she drew her own portrait of the ideal governess and expressed some very sound views on girls' education which were far in advance of her age. The science of teaching really interested Mistress Woolley and she deplored the severe punishments endured by the young. She tells the grim tale of a governess in Dorset who 'called up her maid with whose help she so cruelly chastised a young Gentlewoman for some fault that she died'.

Hannah Woolley begged parents to let their children be lovingly and quietly governed for 'blows are fitter for beasts than for rational creatures'.

She was the first family governess, I should say, to stress the importance of applying different methods of teaching to suit individual children. This was pure commonsense to her. In her own way, Hannah was a pioneer in the field of child psychology.

That queerly named Carolean bluestocking, Bathsua Makin, daughter of the Rector of Southwick, Sussex, and a sister of the famous John Pell, linguist and mathematician, was a contemporary of Hannah's. On account of her great learning, so rare in a woman in the seventeenth century, King Charles I appointed her to be governess to his delicate little daughter, the Princess Elizabeth Stewart. Princess Elizabeth studied feverishly under Mrs Makin. Before she was nine years old she read, wrote and in some measure spoke French, Italian, Latin, Greek and Hebrew. From an engraving by Marshall, Bathsua Makin looks as if she would have been a hard taskmistress. She is an ugly, gnome-like creature with scraped-back hair and a small tucked-in mouth. Her dress is almost Puritan in its severity.

When Princess Elizabeth died in 1650, Mrs Makin's pension of £40 a year, granted by King Charles, was repudiated by Parliament. She earned her living then by taking private pupils. But after life became more normal through the Restoration, she opened a School for Gentlewomen in 1673 at Tottenham

High Cross, making good capital of the fact that she had once been a royal governess. About this time, she published her well-known treatise, *An Essay to Revive the Ancient Education of a Gentlewoman*, writing:

'Merely to teach Gentlewomen to Frisk and Dance, to paint their Faces, to curl their hair, to put on a Whisk, to wear gay Clothes, is not truly to adorn but Adulterate their Bodies. . . . The Tongues ought to be studied, especially the Greek and Hebrew.' But she lacked the courage to break entirely with current teaching fashions and so compromised by including in her school curriculum, 'all those things taught in other schools'. They included making 'Flowers of Coloured Straw and the Building of Houses in Stained Paper', accomplishments secretly despised by her.

Ten years after she had founded her School for Gentlewomen, a little girl of good family was born in Newcastle, who would have been the perfect pupil for Mrs Makin as her one great wish was to learn the ancient languages. The name of this little girl was Elizabeth Elstob, destined to become the most remarkable woman-scholar of her age, and a governess.

Elizabeth Elstob: The Saxon Lady 1683-1756

On the death of her parents young Elizabeth Elstob was placed in the care of her uncle, the Reverend Charles Elstob, Prepandary of Canterbury Cathedral, who was 'no friend to women's learning'. He disapproved strongly of his niece's bluestocking tendencies and when she asked him at the age of ten if she could learn French, he held up his hands in horror. One language, her own, was all a woman should know, he told Elizabeth sharply. Fortunately, her good Aunt Elstob was on her side and helped her niece to acquire some French. After French Elizabeth struggled on, alone, to learn Latin, Greek and, finally, Saxon.

Elizabeth had a brother, ten years her senior, whom she

adored. In 1702, when he was appointed Vicar of St Swithin and St Mary Bothaw in the City of London, she went to house-keep for him in Bush Lane, near London Stone. The years that followed were very happy for Elizabeth; they were the only happy years she knew in her long chequered life. During this time, inspired by William, who always referred to her as 'the dear and tireless companion of my studies', Elizabeth became known as a brilliant scholar and writer. The relationship be-tween this devoted pair recalls that other charming partner-ship of a literary brother and sister – William Wordsworth and his Dorothy. A favourite pastime of Elizabeth's was to copy old manuscripts and some beautiful specimens of her work have been preserved. Ralph Thoresby, the well-known Leeds topographer, who often visited her, has recorded how his hostess 'drew and painted curiously'.

It was not long before the Elstobs were attracting eminent men of learning to their quiet vicarage. Through the narrow, squalid streets of the city darkened by the projecting eaves of old timbered houses, they came; soberly dressed, in coats of snuff-brown and mole-grey, with their heads bent in deep argument. Amongst them were such renowned scholars as Doctor Hickes and Brome the Antiquarian. When Elizabeth published her first book, *An English Saxon Homily on the Birth-day of St Gregory*, in 1709, she was affectionately nick-named the Saxon Lady by her friends.

Nichols, a contemporary writer, who knew Elizabeth, has recorded in his *Literary Anecdotes*, that she was a plain young woman. On the contrary, her only portrait, inserted in the capital letter 'G', with which the English version of her *A Homily on the Birthday of St Gregory* opens, shows the head of an attractive girl, with dark curly hair, in a low-necked dress. Her eyes, under fine, well-marked eye-brows are full of charm and intelligence.

As the queen of a select circle of scholarly men, Elizabeth's reign was brief. In 1715, her delicate and over-worked brother contracted consumption and died. He left his beloved sister at the youthful age of thirty-one for a scholar, penniless. For a while Elizabeth struggled on to launch her second book, *A Saxon Homilarium*. Without William to press patrons into financing its publication, she saw that the most ambitious and dearest of her literary projects was doomed to failure. Unable to earn her daily bread by writing and faced with the prospect of being thrown into prison for debts, incurred by her brother's illness and death, Elizabeth took the only course open to her and vanished.

For twelve years nothing was heard in London of the Saxon Lady. Far away, in the old market town of Evesham in Worcestershire, Elizabeth had opened a small school and was teaching. In rural England, learning had been brought practically to a standstill for lack of patronage from the landed gentry. That warm love of knowledge for its own sake, so glowingly characteristic of the Tudor Age, had grown cold or survived only in a few intellectually-minded homes. The Civil War was much to blame as it had emptied many a rich man's purse and county magnates could not afford to found, or endow, grammar schools for the needy and poor. The only source of education for village children, was the dame's school where they learnt their letters from the Hornbook or Bible. In his poem, *The Schoolmistress* (1754), William Shenstone the 'landskip' gardener and poet, has vividly described how :

> ' In every village mark'd with a little spire,
>   Embowered in trees, and hardly known to fame,
>   There dwells in lowly shed, and mean attire,
>   A matron old, whom we school-mistris name . . .'

These old matrons in their russet stoles and mutch-caps hold as important a place as any in the slow evolution of mass education through the ages. Amongst them, there must often have been some poor but intellectually rich gentlewoman, like Elizabeth Elstob, who satisfied her desire to keep learning alive in the seventeenth century by becoming a village school-

dame. Elizabeth's work was hard and lovely though Avon-
side was and sweet-scented with apple blossom and plum in
spring, she had little time to enjoy it. As little time, too, to
snatch a meal during her long day's teaching. It was Tindal,
Evesham's well-known historian, who wrote that Mistress
Elstob's school was kept 'with great success doubtless to
her scholars but little emolument to herself, her weekly
stipend with each pupil was, as I am credibly informed, at
first only a groat'.

All the same, Elizabeth struggled on even when afflicted by
what she called 'her old Nervous Fever from which I despair
of ever being free; it affects my Head, Eyes and Hands, so
much as to make me almost incapable of writing'. This fever
must have been an acute form of neuritis.

The years passed, uneventfully, for Elizabeth in Evesham,
where the talk was always of vegetable growing, of Pershore
plums, and 'sparrer grass', but never of Saxon. Still she was
not without friends. At Stanton, close by, there was lively
Mrs Chapone, wife of the vicar and mother-in-law of the celebrated authoress, Hester Mulso, who had known Elizabeth
in London. Over at Campden was George Ballard, the scholarly habit-maker, very busy writing his famous *Memoirs of
Learned Ladies*. Ballard was only twenty-nine, the Saxon Lady
fifty-three, when they first met; but they liked one another
immediately. Elizabeth asked Ballard to visit her at Evesham,
warning him that, 'You will see a poor little contemptible
old maid generally Vapour'd up to the ears, but very Chearful when she meets with Agreeable Conversation'.

It was the exchange of stimulating ideas with people of her
own high intellectual attainments that she missed most and
needed, fatigued by the ceaseless babble of children. Later she
went over to Campden and so enjoyed her stay with Ballard
in that lovely Cotswold wool town that she apologised pa-
thetically for having had 'too much Loquacity, I do assure
you it is only among those I esteem as my best Friends that I
put now on those Gaities'.

Through Mrs Chapone, Elizabeth came to meet the kind-hearted and charming Ann Granville living with her mother at Gloucester. Miss Granville was connected to many great aristocratic families of the day and informed her widowed sister, Mary Pendarves (later the famous Mrs Delany), that the once well-known Saxon Lady had become a humble village school-dame. Immediately, Mrs Pendarves began to busy herself in finding her sister's protegée more congenial work.

Gracefully, she petitioned Her Majesty, Queen Caroline, to interest herself in 'a once renowned Lady living in complete penury'. When the Queen heard that the lady in question was none other than Elizabeth Elstob, the Saxon scholar, she not only promised to allow her £20 a year but added graciously, 'as she is so proper to be mistress of a boarding-school for young ladies of higher rank, I will, instead of an allowance, send her £100 now and repeat the same at the end of every five years'.

But Her Majesty had not reckoned with Elizabeth's altruistic spirit. As the sister of a hard-working London slum parson, who had sacrificed his life to the cause of educating the poor, Elizabeth knew that her Evesham scholars needed her services far more than the elegantly hooped and powdered little ladies, suggested by Queen Caroline. Besides, she told Ballard, 'Having met with a great deal of Friendship & Generosity from the Good Ladies in this place, I should think it a greatest piece of Ingratitude to neglect the Dear Little ones committed to my Care.'

So Elizabeth refused Queen Caroline's patronage; nor did she accept the post of Head of a Charity School when offered by Lady Elizabeth Hastings. Again she replied proudly to Ballard's criticisms: 'As to your objections to the meaness of my scholars, I assure you, Sir, I shou'd think it as Glorious an Employment to instruct Poor Children as to teach the Children of the Greatest Monarch.'

Never once, in her long life, did Elizabeth Elstob make a tragedy of her deliberately chosen vocation. Once she had renounced all thought of pursuing her Saxon studies, she dedicated herself wholeheartedly to teaching the young.

But Mrs Pendarves persisted in her efforts to place Mrs Elstob in a better position. Soon George Ballard was hearing from his friend of 'an offer from the Duke & Duchess of Portland to teach their children to Read, with an allowance of a Sallary of Thirty Pounds a year . . . there are only two little Ladys to teach at present, the eldest not yet four years old, and the little Marquis not one . . . neither my best Friends nor myself could have wished for a more happy & Honourable Situation for me'.

While Elizabeth had almost accepted the idea of exchanging her rustic schoolroom for a ducal one – she was getting on in years and lonely – *the Elstobian affair*, as Mary Pendarves described it, dragged on. Surprisingly, Lord and Lady Oxford, the Duchess of Portland's parents, had raised objections to Mrs Elstob's appointment as governess to their grand-children on the grounds that she did not speak good conversational French. Poor Elizabeth began to doubt herself if she was the right person to become governess to a duchess. These doubts were shared by her old friend, Brome, the Antiquarian, who wrote bluntly to Ballard:

'I am glad the Saxon Lady is to leave Evesham for a better Place. I hope she has seen so much of the world, as since her Dedication of A. S. Grammar, she may have other thoughts; but if they should continue the same, desire her, conjure her, to secret them, because to my certain knowledge they are different and will be displeasing to the great Lady's (the Duchess of Portland) Friends, with whom I have the honour to be acquainted.'

Brome knew that real scholarship like Elizabeth's was little appreciated in fashionable society. Though the Duchess was well educated, with a warm heart, she had 'that passion for collecting', so characteristic of eighteenth century ladies. Her love of natural history had begun young and anything rare or curious attracted her strongly. After an early marriage, she began to collect strange plants and flowers, exotic birds, scarlet japan and the new blue and white china; above all, shells. In time, she was to acquire the celebrated Portland Vase.

Her favourite hobby was *turning;* she was highly skilled in turning jet, ivory and amber as well as wood, and had a room set apart at Bulstrode, her country home, for this work. She was not a true intellectual to be impressed by great learning like Elizabeth's. But she still wanted her as governess. When, to please her parents, it was decided to engage a French master to teach her daughters, Mrs Pendarves hurriedly wrote off to her sister in Gloucester, to say how imprudent it would be for Mrs Elstob to refuse another offer coming from the Duchess, especially:

'When no fatigue will be placed on her, but all imaginable care will be taken of her ... all she (the Duchess) requires and hopes of Mrs Elstob is to instruct her children in the principles of religion, and cultivate their minds as far as their capacity will allow, to keep them company in the house, and when her strength and health permit to Take the Air with them. All this she is well qualified to do, and it would be a sincere joy to me to have our worthy Duchess possest of so valuable a person.' (Bulstrode, 12th December 1738)

Away in Bath, taking the waters for her failing health, Elizabeth Elstob wrote enthusiastically to Ann Granville of the two long letters she had received from Mrs Pendarves, delineating the charming character of her future employer, the Duchess. Her mind was made up at last. She would become a ducal governess though she still considered herself unworthy of the position.

By Christmas, *the Elstobian affair* was quite fixed and the Duchess of Portland very much satisfied at having secured such a worthy woman to educate her children, Ann Granville was informed by her sister.

In July 1739, soon after the birth of the Duchess's fourth child, Lady Margaret Cavendish Bentinck, whom Elizabeth Elstob was to love best of all her pupils, she took up her appointment. If she had been younger and less of a literary eccentric, accustomed to living alone with her books, the Saxon Lady might have been as happy among 'the sweet delights of Bulstrode' as Selina Trimmer was happy at Chatsworth, fifty years later.

At Bulstrode with its slender Nubian cranes and brown hares fed with scraps on the lawn, its aviary, and parkland where curious wild animals roamed, the Duchess treated her distinguished governess with courtesy and was kindness itself when they met. But she rarely visited the schoolroom. Her children were not with her constantly like the Duchess of Devonshire's. At least, not until they were grown-up. Her two elder daughters, affectionately nick-named the 'Twopennies', came to her at five in the afternoon and then, after 'an hour's jumping' were sent back to their apartments. There were no great balls or gambling parties staged at Bulstrode, as there were at Devonshire House. Her Grace of Portland preferred to be surrounded by a small circle of intimate friends, headed by her beloved Mrs Pendarves whom she called 'Penny'. With them, she studied rare prints of bird and wild animal life; did elaborate feather-work and picked shells. The intricacies of a dull dead language like Saxon held no charm for the Duchess with her love of the fantastic. Poor Mrs Elstob came to see less and less of her.

Sadly she wrote to gentle Ann Granville, now contemplating marriage with a Mr Dewes in Gloucester: 'I want nothing here to make my happiness complete as this world can make it, but the pleasure of seeing Mrs Pendarves oftener, who is entirely engrossed by Her Grace. I can send you nothing new from hence; Mrs Pendarves can do it better, who hears and sees more than I do . . . We begin to talk of going to Bulstrode, where I long to be because I hope to have the honour of more of her Grace's company – for it is impossible to have any of it here.' (Whitehall, 6th May 1740)

But Bulstrode was no better than Whitehall. The Duchess spent long hours inside her *turning-room*. She was busy on a new 'Gothic cell' surrounded by her intimates. Elizabeth was still odd man out. Accustomed to loneliness and indifferent to whether her work was appreciated or not, she turned to the children, to Lady Betty and Lady Harriet and the tiny Marquis of Titchfield. On seeing the new governess, he had stretched out his fat little arms and gurgled 'Tob'. And so, Tob she became, instead of the Saxon Lady.

Soon she was writing to George Ballard, far away in Campden: 'My charming little Ladies take up my time so entirely that I have not the least leisure to do anything from the time they rise till they go to bed, they are so constantly with me, except when they are with her Grace, which is not long at a time.'

It was not long before Lady Betty, a lively intelligent child who had not known a single letter of her alphabet before her learned governess's arrival, 'already knows them all, can spell and read very prettily, and can say some little Poems, and a great deal of the Catechism she knew not one word before'.

At least, Elizabeth Elstob had found love in one room at Bulstrode – the schoolroom. Her friends, George Ballard and Mrs Chapone, might worry over her being nothing more now than an elderly governess, tucked away in one corner of a vast ducal establishment, rarely seen and seldom visited. They had forgotten that the Saxon Lady was always happy when imparting knowledge to budding minds.

What of her leisure? they asked in letters; or her Saxon studies? It was far too late to recall the long forgotten delights of literary life to Elizabeth Elstob. The Saxon Lady had bid adieu to creative work when her brother, William, lay dying, in his parsonage. In her homely, brown worsted gown which had been Ballard's farewell present to her, and wearing always her own hand-knitted, thick woollen stockings, Elizabeth continued to live at Whitehall or Bulstrode as she had once lived, solitary, at Evesham.

'I have less time than ever I had in my life to command because it is not my own,' she informed George Ballard adding in another letter to Mrs Dewes (Ann Granville that was), 'My dear little Charmers allow me very little leisure'.

She genuinely loved children, for in this same letter she describes how Lady Betty and she did lessons together: 'She learns exceedingly well, and loves her books and me entirely; nor is she more happy than when she is with me, and we study together, even by candlelight, like two old folk.'

It is a charming picture of two charming people; the absorbed child and devoted governess. Did it matter so much to Elizabeth that the erudite phraseology of her *Homily on the Birthday of St Gregory* had been changed for the simple, short sentences of *The Tale of the Turtle* or *Molly Mog* spelt out in a childish treble?

Mrs Elstob fell ill now; so ill that the busy but warm-hearted Duchess thought she might die. Elizabeth's letters to Ballard dwindle and almost peter out. In 1710, she wrote to him: 'Pray let us continue to see one another if Possible'; then sadly, regretfully, 'Alas! my acquaintance and interest is reduced to a very narrow compass'. What her friends had feared had taken place. Her few remaining memories of literary fame once known in a London vicarage had been completely erased from her mind by childish prattle and two figures, the one of a beloved brother, the other of a clever girl, queen of a select circle, become mere ghosts.

But her pupils' affection never failed her and when she temporarily lost the use of her right hand her 'sweet Ladys' – as she always called them – wrote her letters for her. By this time, Lord Titchfield was doing extremely well at Westminster and Lady Margaret Cavendish Bentinck had joined her two older sisters in the Portland schoolroom. So the years passed till the poor Saxon Lady became so crippled by rheumatism that she could only hobble about with a stick. In 1753, Mrs Delany reports her failing health to her sister: 'I am just come down from Mrs Elstob. She is wrapt up in her young lords and ladies, and I believe has no thought of

The Village Dame

THE
ENGLISH-SAXON
GRAMMAR.

RAMMAR is the Art of Speaking and Writing, truly and properly. In Speaking we use certain Signs, which are necessary to discover our Thoughts to one another. These Signs, are Sound, and Voice.

But besides, Sound, and Voice, by which we are able to converse with one another when present; There are other Signs have been invented, where these Sounds cannot be heard, to supply the want of them in such manner, as that we may both converse with one another at a distance, and communicate our Thoughts to future Ages.

The first of these Signs belongs properly to Speech, or unwritten Discourse. The latter are made use of in Writing.

Hence the *Greeks*, from whom we receiv'd the first Rudiments of this Art, have deliver'd down to us the

Names

Elizabeth Elstob

quitting them till they disperse into homes of their own; and, indeed, she is too infirm to undertake any fresh change now.' (Bulstrode, 9th December.)

Poor Elizabeth! Her fingers were far too stiff to hold her beloved quill and her sight was almost gone. No more could she draw and paint curiously. If she had, the door would have been opened to the Duchess's dressing-room, known as 'The Hive', and its occupants, that charmed circle seated inside, the Hivites. The Duchess had been joined recently in The Hive by her two elder daughters both interested in doing ornamental arts like their mother. Lady Betty and Lady Harriet were lively, pleasant girls, very 'easy in their manner and under no restraint before the Duchess than to watch her looks and motions and instantly obey them', wrote Mrs Delany who had just arrived on one of her long periodical visits to Bulstrode. Lady Betty and she began to make an elaborate shell-lustre for the Duchess. What did the Saxon Lady think of this new occupation of her ex-pupil? Confined to her room, upstairs, she sat, surrounded by piles of dusty books, in her tall wing-chair. Sometimes there came the sound of a light step outside her door, a gentle knock, and then little Lady Margaret would appear to read aloud to her old governess. Sometimes, there came Lady Betty, to show off her latest drawing – the copy of a rare fish by Ehret, which she had found in one of Mrs Delany's books.

How did the child find time to do all 'these ingenious works', Elizabeth wondered, and said so in confidence to Mrs Dewes. But for the child, herself, she had no criticism, only a smile and nod of welcome. The household thought of her as a crabbed old lady, best left alone in her study, but to her dear children she was always their loving Tob.

In the spring of 1755 young Lord Edward Cavendish succumbed to scarlet fever and soon the entire Portland family was struck down, besides many members of the household. To the great grief of her parents, delicate Lady Margaret did not recover. No one dared tell her old governess, ill herself

49

at the time, of the child's tragic death. From Spring Gardens, London, where she had taken a house, Mary Delany gives the latest Portland news as usual to her sister, Mrs Dewes: 'Mrs Elstob is gradually drawing towards that happy repose which we may presume so good a woman may obtain'. (24th May 1756)

Elizabeth had been told at last of Lady Margaret's death. The news shook her deeply and she did not long survive the beloved child. Although Mrs Delany paid many visits to her sick-room, and urged her, at the Duchess's request to call in a physician, she would have none; nor would she seek spiritual consolation from any clergyman. At the last, she fell into a coma and died on Sunday, 3rd June. She was buried at St Margaret's Church, Westminster.

Lord Titchfield, her handsome, talented boy, never forgot that he owed his fine intellectual training to his 'dear Tob' and repaid her by taking one University honour after another. 'I can safely say without boasting or partiality he is an admirable scholar for his age which is not fifteen,' his governess had written once proudly to Mrs Dewes.

This was high praise coming from the first woman to make a direct contribution to English scholarship; the woman whose indomitable courage had carried the flickering torch of culture for women, another stage forward, at a time when social conditions were so adverse to learning for women. During the years that she was governess to the Duchess of Portland, Elizabeth Elstob learned, as Fanny Burney learned later when she was in royal service, how chary the great ladies of the early eighteenth century were of giving their patronage to female education. It was sad that Mrs Elstob's best friend, Mrs Chapone of Stanton, was not considered to be of sufficient social standing to be invited to Bulstrode. In fact, dear Mrs Elstob received a severe rap over the knuckles from Mrs Delany for suggesting such a thing. Mrs Delany knew best on matters of social behaviour. Nor did Elizabeth gain the Duchess's permission for her other friend,

George Ballard, to dedicate his *Memoirs of Learned Ladies* to Her Grace.

'I am sorry to tell you the choice you have made for the Honour of the Females was the wrong'st subject you could pitch upon,' she wrote to Ballard. 'For you can come into no company of Ladies or Gentlemen, where you shall not hear an open and Vehement exclamation against Learned Women, and by those women that read much themselves, to what purpose they know best . . . The prospect I have of the next age is a melancholy one to me who wish Learning might flourish to the end of the world, both in men and women, but I shall not live to see it.'

But the tide was turning; turning towards a fuller and kinder recognition of learning for women. In 1697, Mary Astell had published *A Serious Proposal to the Ladies*, pleading that their sex were capable of nobler things than 'pursuing butterflies and trifles'.

Fifty years later, there came a complete *volte-face* from society leaders like witty Mrs Elizabeth Montague, Mrs Carter and Fanny Boscawen. Instead of spending long hours in stringing pearls or picking shells, they turned their attention to establishing salons for blue-stockings and were even named 'blues', themselves. Thus female learning was made fashionable at last. Elizabeth Elstob had not lived in vain although, to keep her independence, she had been forced to earn her living first as a humble village school-dame, then as a family governess but never as the brilliant woman of letters she was by right. Still, in her own way she had triumphed by sowing the intellectual seed, so beloved by her, in young and fruitful ground.

CHAPTER THREE

The Eighteenth Century Governess

'To communicate her Knowledge and Virtue requires no ordinary talents and exertions. To accomplish such an end a governess in the first place should be a Prodigy of Virtue. Like Charity "she should suffer long and be kind". She should love her pupils as her daughters and possess great knowledge embellished with taste. She should appear always lovely and always inviting, knowing the best Books.'

REV JOHN BENNETT *Letters to a Young Lady* 1789

Though it was fashionable in the eighteenth century to send girls to boarding-schools, little attention was paid at them to their health. Bedrooms were small, two to three pupils often sleeping in one bed, and the food provided insufficient for healthy, young appetites. In consequence, many girls died from consumption called 'a putrid fever'. For this reason, wealthy parents preferred to keep a resident governess, who first taught their daughters then acted as their chaperones. This kind of early Georgian, schoolroom education was supplemented at a later stage by lessons from visiting masters in French, Singing, and Dancing. On the whole, the eighteenth century girl was not taught the classics like her Tudor forbear. In Samuel Richardson's novel *Clarissa Harlowe*, first published in 1747, Mrs Judith Norton is an excellent example of the period governess. She is described as 'a woman of great purity and discretion who had a principle share in the education of Clarissa'.

Her pupil's brother, the 'arrogant James' referred to Mrs Norton as 'Goody Norton'. Samuel Richardson makes it quite clear that Clarissa's friends admired her skill in music, her fine needlework, and her deep reading no less than her moral superiority. Clarissa was a past mistress in the art of elocution and read aloud admirably. She had 'no tone, no whine', and her emphasis was always well-placed. Poetry read by her, was poetry indeed. She wrote a neat flowing hand, she spelt and punctuated correctly. All these accomplishments reflect on Mrs Norton's excellent training.

Calligraphy was carefully studied through the century, a writing-master teaching the well-bred girl the art of 'making, holding, and managing the Pen'. A famous writing master of the day was George Shelley whose *Alphabets, in all the Hands*, printed in 1710, was studied by governesses. Eighteenth century copy-books are full of charm. One called *The Compendious Emblematist* (1750) has a coloured plate of a coy Mermaid gazing into a Mirror; below her is a specimen copy of the letter 'M'. On the opposite page are printed these lines:

> 'Sweet the Mermaid's Voice and Fair her Face,
> But certain Death attends her soft Embrace.'

Besides these copy-books, special writing-sheets could be bought at the fancy stationer's which were part and parcel of a governess's professional equipment; they were coloured and cost a penny or two per sheet. Their centres, which were left empty, could be filled in by a pupil in her best hand-writing, signed and then presented to her proud father or mother at some suitable time like Christmas. Pretty geographical cards, complete with 'Directions for playing an Entertaining Game' that were the popular forerunners of *The Counties of England*, made geography almost as much fun for the governess as for the pupil. In fact, there was no end to the number of instructive little manuals that flooded the eighteenth century schoolroom. Delightfully printed with hand-coloured plates, they are now highly prized as 'collector pieces'.

It was during the eighteenth century that we first hear of the word 'schoolroom'. The actual date for its appearance is given by the editors of the *New English Dictionary* as 1775, though the resident governess had been established in family life for well over two hundred years before. In the *Anecdotes of Mary: or the Good Governess*, printed in 1795, I found one of the few descriptions there are of the eighteenth century schoolroom. But even in this case, as in others, it was only the 'nursery' that had been transformed into Mary's 'schoolroom'.

'When Lady S – 's toilet was finished, Mary went to supper, and from there to her nursery, but how surprised was she to find it quite altered. Her play-room which before was almost empty, was now furnished with a bookcase, writing table, drawing-desk, gloves, and a harpsichord. In the room where she was accustomed to sleep was a little bed, placed by the side of a large white dimity one. She presently guessed what all this meant, and turning to the maid who accompanied her, she hastily cried, "For God's sake put me to bed that I may not see her till Morning". All her good maid, Ann, replied was: "Oh, if you mean your governess, ma'am, you must make haste, for 'tis now half past seven, and she is to come at eight".'

A room especially equipped for the governess does not seem to have been thought necessary much before Victorian times. Governesses invariably slept with their pupils during the eighteenth century. Kindly she-dragons, they preserved them from all physical harm.

In her *Memoirs of a Highland Lady*, Elizabeth Grant describes how she and her little sisters 'slept in one large room at the top of the new part of the House' with their governess, Miss Elphick. Each girl had 'a little white-curtained bed, made to fit into the slope of the roof in its own corner . . . The middle of the room with its window, fire-place, toilettes, and book tables, made our common dressing-room.'

Miss Elphick began the day by jumping out of bed at six o'clock in the morning 'throwing on her clothes with the haste of one escaping from a house on fire; she wiped her face and hands, and smoothed her cropped hair and her toilette was over . . . Miss Elphick considered ten minutes quite sufficient for any young lady to give to her toilette upon weekdays'.

The Grant schoolroom had also been the nursery, curtained and carpeted anew. It had a high fender, two hanging bookcases and six framed maps on the wall. One map on Mercator's projection they could never understand, said Elizabeth in her Journal.

It was considered bad manners to be rude to the governess during the eighteenth century: nor was she slighted in public by her pupils like the Victorian governess. Miss Maria Edgeworth informed her readers how 'in her time, the Governess was no longer treated as an Upper Servant but as a Gentlewoman'. In the recently published *Heber Letters* (1782–1832) the Reverend Reginald Heber, Rector of Malpas and Parson of Hodnet, was told by his sister in a letter dated 1798, that:

'We will make all the enquiries we can after a governess for little Mary, but such as are in every respect eligible are difficult to be met with and their terms very high. There are plenty of emigrant ladies, some of the rank of Viscountess, to be had, but I think you would not prefer a French-woman, and I am sure would not take a Roman-Catholic into your House. We have just hired a governess for Mary Ann, her wages or salary is to be forty guineas a year, her washing is done at home or paid for, and she is to eat at their own table. She undertakes to instruct her pupil in English, French, Geography, Music, Writing & Arithmetic. The wages are now, it seems, thought low, fifty or sixty pounds or guineas being frequently given.'

The eighteenth century governess most resembles the mediaeval 'maistresse', known to Chaucer. It was her duty, first and foremost, to preserve her pupils' virgin bloom as eighteenth century man desired the female sex to be full of exquisite sensibility like Clarissa Harlowe. Quite often, too, on the premature death of a young mother in child-birth, the governess took complete charge in a country house. Then, her pupils looked to her to supply them with love as well as with schoolroom knowledge.

For months on end, they would live alone in those lovely houses that stood, isolated, in romantic parkland, all over

Georgian England; houses now mouldering away into tragic ruin or vanished completely. Parents were often away in London or doing the Grand Tour of Europe. In their absence, the governess gave orders to obedient and respectful servants; drove with her charges in the lumbering family chariot to church; or accompanied them out walking when they were attended either by young Sambo, a blackamoor page, or Old Thomas, a family retainer. Under the governess's eye the lap-dogs were washed and much precious china. Needlework had to be done and a little gardening. During the long winter days a Shell Grotto was devised or an elaborate Paper-work Screen made for the Long Gallery. The education of the village children was undertaken at this time by the squire's wife assisted by her daughters and the governess.

At Tallentire in the county of Cumberland, little Catherine and Mary Stewart-Browne with their governess, Miss Wragge, known as 'a clever and progressive lady' taught in the village dame's school every day and organised 'readings' for the local farmers.

Exercising such authority in the house and schoolroom, it is much to the credit of the eighteenth century governess how rarely she was disliked by servants or pupils. There is one governess, though, dark and nameless, who was so consumed by jealousy, that she is reputed to have starved the beautiful heiress, Grace Naylor, to death in her room, at Hurstmonceaux. Her ghost still haunts the Lady's Bower.

Lady Anne Lindsay, famous as the authoress of that charming ballad, *Auld Robin Gray*, has described her Scottish schoolroom life vividly, in what she named her *Vagrant Scraps*. Her governess, a Miss Henrietta Cumming, nick-named Hennie the Sylph, had been found by her mother, Lady Balcarres, weeping and painting butterflies in an Edinburgh garret. She wept because she was not placed in that sphere of life to which she rightly belonged. To mend this sad injustice, Lady Balcarres took Hennie back with her to the great Castle of Balcarres, rising beside the Firth of Forth. 'Behold her, then, settled at Balcarres, the least little woman that ever was seen for nothing,' wrote Lady Anne, her pupil. 'Fantastic in her dress and naïve in her manners beyond what was natural at her time of life, her countenance was pretty, her shape neat and nice.' For the rest of her life, Hennie the Sylph made her home with the Lindsay family. 'The old house-dog was as likely to be turned from his mat, and left to shiver in the cold, as Henrietta to be sent away from our chimney-corner because our education was completed,' recorded Lady Anne. On the death of old Lord Balcarres, Hennie found she had been left a small annuity. Her gratitude knew no bounds.

Besides being affectionately treated, the eighteenth century governess was honoured at her death. In some quiet little country churchyard, records of faithful service by one who was more a family friend than a paid employee, can be found marking some crumbling headstone, elegantly engraved. At Great Durnford Church, near Salisbury, for instance, one tablet dated 1811 commemorates the death of a much-loved, old governess, born on 18th April 1737, who was in the employ of the Harris family for more than fifty years.

' This Tablet is placed by the Honble Katherine Gertrude Robinson and her sister Louisa Margaret Harris Inhabitants of the adjoining Manor House. To the memory of Mrs Gout, who was chosen by their Parents to superintend their Education in the early part of their lives. From the careful manner in which she executed this trust Mrs Gout was considered by them and their family during a period of more than fifty years as a most faithful and affectionate friend and for this reason as well as from her unaffected piety and the strict integrity of her character truly deserving of this mark of their esteem and regard.'

The wording may be a trifle pompous but the tribute is sincere. On a slab in the north transept of Salisbury Cathedral, written in a beautiful, flowing type of lettering, one reads:

> Here lies the body of
> Anne Dear Widow who
> dyed Wednesday the 27
> of April Anno Domini 1720

The most famous mistress
in the west of England
for well educating and
instructing young ladys
and gentlewomen.

A distinguished governess, indeed, to be buried inside a Cathedral.

From this background of civilised country-house life found in England from about 1750 onwards, came Maria Edgeworth, the novelist, who made her own special contribution to female education. Actually, Maria's home was in Ireland where she was brought up by her father, Richard Lovell Edgeworth, a brilliant man but eccentric. He was married three times and Maria helped him educate his large family as a girl in her teens. She was a born teacher like Elizabeth Elstob. In *Practical Education*, written in collaboration with her father in 1798, Maria airs her views on how a young girl should be brought up in the family schoolroom. She headed her chapter, 'Female Accomplishments, Masters, and Governesses'. Maria Edgeworth was very much influenced by the new methods of education, being put forward by the French writer and philosopher, Jean Jacques Rousseau. She redressed many of his theories for English parents. She drew her own portrait, too, of the ideal period governess. Instead of an endless train of dancing-masters, French tutors, Italian maestros, etc, instructing a pupil, Maria urged parents to appoint 'one superior person of enlarged and philosophic mind', who would be placed in sole charge of the schoolroom. This lady would not be chosen because she was 'a mistress of the arts, a performer in music, a paintress, a linguist, or a poetess but,' Maria stressed, 'because she had a steadiness of purpose, freedom from prejudice, and that species of integrity which would justify a parent in trusting a child to her care'. This paragon of all the teaching virtues was to receive the princely salary of £300 per annum for three years during which time, she would be able to put something by against her retirement. She would be able to give of her best, then, freed from financial worry. Unknowingly, Maria Edgeworth had drawn the portrait of an actual governess, living at the time. She was Miss Selina Trimmer, who secure in her 'upper bow' room at Chatsworth but securer still in the affections of a lovely Duchess and her pupils, the clever Cavendish children, was a unique specimen of the perfect family governess, not only in the eighteenth century but of all time.

Miss Selina Trimmer: La Fée Vigèle
1765-1829

When the Dowager Lady Spencer tactfully suggested to her daughter Georgiana, the lovely and gay Duchess of Devonshire, that a governess should be engaged to take charge of her two small daughters and that she knew just the right person for the situation, the Duchess asked her, who was the young woman so eminently suitable? On hearing that it was the eldest daughter of one of her mother's oldest and most trusted friends, Mrs Trimmer of Brentford, well-known for her *Moral Tales*, the Duchess smiled and agreed it was an excellent choice. So Lady Spencer got to work.

But her task was not easy. Mrs Trimmer was nervous of letting her daughter Selina go to Devonshire House, that notorious Whig household. To begin with, it was a curious *ménage à trois* that Selina would find on arrival. For some time now, Lady Elizabeth Foster, daughter of Lord Bristol and wife of John Thomas Foster, an Irish squire, whom she had left, had been living on intimate terms with the Duke and Duchess.* Then there was the Duchess herself. It was common gossip that she turned night into day, never rising before 4 pm in the afternoon and retiring to her room about 3 am. She had a wild passion for entertaining, the passport for the

---

* Lady Elizabeth Foster (alias Lady Liz or Bess) made her home at Devonshire House from 1781 at Georgiana's own request. She had two children by the Duke, Caro St Jules and Augustus Clifford.

entrée to her parties being not so much the possession of blue blood and impeccable morals as brilliance of conversation, plus wit and a love for gambling. People came and went, unchecked at Devonshire House and no kind of routine was kept. Mrs Trimmer, who conducted her Brentford household with the utmost regularity and, like Lady Spencer, was a great believer 'in Method', was worried. But as Lady Spencer kept pointing out, Selina's life lay sealed within the secure walls of a schoolroom. A room, moreover, which was to be *her* kingdom, for the Duchess had promised her complete authority over her children. Eventually, the Dowager's tact, coupled with Mrs Trimmer's firm belief in Selina's innate good sense and high moral standards won the day. Miss Trimmer accepted the position of governess to the Ladies Georgiana and Harriet Cavendish.

At twenty-one, with jet-black eyes, Selina was considered to be very like her 'unaffected, mild, pleasing and placid' mother. These are excellent traits for a young governess. She had been well trained, too.

'In order to relieve me of fatigue, and give me leisure for writing, my eldest daughter has chiefly educated the younger children,' wrote chubby Mrs Trimmer, who always wore a ruched mob cap and had a warm heart.

Thus teaching began early for Selina under her mother's admirable tuition. Mrs Trimmer had published several books based on lessons which she had given her own children. Her charming *History of the Robins* had early established her as the Beatrix Potter of the eighteenth century schoolroom and she was one of the first children's writers to say that animals should be treated more kindly: this was quite a revolutionary idea in her day.

One morning, then, in 1786, a handsome coach on whose glossy panels were painted the Devonshire coat of arms, drew up before a wooden door, set in a high brick wall, in Windmill Lane, Brentford. Behind this wall, stood the pretty, double-bowed villa in which Selina had been born and which she was now preparing to leave. With a last-minute blessing from her cheerful rotund mother and many hand-wavings and cries of farewell from her brothers and sisters gathered round to see her off, Selina drove away to London.

She did not find life easy at first at Devonshire House. For she had been engaged by the astute Lady Spencer as a kind of secret agent to report to her privately whether her adored grandchildren were being brought up in the correct Spencer family traditions of high thinking and plain living. Selina had been warned against the Duchess's famous charm and had steeled herself to meet and to remain totally unaffected by it. Hardly, though, had she been installed with her mother's favourite grammar books, her globes, and her scruples in London's most talked-about house when she fell a victim to her youngest pupil's droll tongue and chubby charm.

A miniature of this very engaging child by John Russell, RA, shows her sitting up in a muslin dress with her tiny alert eyes, twinkling under the frill of a gauzy mob-cap. Imbued from infancy with a strong sense of justice, she soon complained to her new governess, 'you treat me like a beggar's child but my sister as a fine lady'.

Selina's heart was touched by such juvenile frankness and foreseeing a battle after her own heart she told the Duchess that 'Lady Harriet walks about very slowly in the room when told to do anything and says, "she won't put herself in a hurry for anybody".' But, drawing herself up, Selina continued, 'Lady Harriet knows I will have the *upper hand*'.

Of course, Selina triumphed and very soon Lady Harriet or Hary-o, as she was called, had given in to the authoritative voice in charge of her energetic and self-willed small person.

When the Duchess went abroad in 1789, Selina was left in complete control. 'My mother will always help you, Selina,' said Her Grace, 'but it is to *you* I must entrust my children.' The Duchess was to be kept as well informed as possible of her daughters' health in those days of long-delayed posts and dawdling couriers.

The first letter that Selina wrote to the Duchess was on the occasion of Hary-o's birthday. It is very characteristic of her: 'I dare say you think me very sulky, my dear Madam, but you will get nothing but dabs from me now. The young ladies are quite well and all you can wish them to be. I shall not say very much about dear Lady Harriet for I am afraid I am partial but I do think both in mind and body there was never a more promising child, she is in high spirits at being the Queen of the Day and directing it with all kind of droll ideas.' (29th August 1789)

Far away in France, Georgiana Devonshire must have smiled to herself. Selina partial? What an admission! Oh, but she must see them, her darling children. She was never happy when away from them long. So it was planned that her mother should bring Miss Trimmer and her charges out to Brussels to join her.

On 4th March 1790, Georgiana wrote to G, her eldest daughter, that their complicated travelling arrangements had been completed at last. She enclosed her dearest G a list of towns through which they would drive. Selina was to point them out on a map. Miss Trimmer was only too delighted to co-operate with the Duchess. She had been much taken by a suggestion of Her Grace to enliven her children's lessons, writing back: 'I like the scheme of the magic-lantern; I think it may be made very instructive and entertaining.'

In the eighteenth century schoolroom the magic-lantern was what television is today – a thrilling new invention! Selina's mother was a strong advocate of its use in lessons. The Cavendish children's education was supervised by their imaginative mother and there is no evidence that young Georgiana and Hary-o were taught elegant accomplishments like Shellwork and Filagree. Only once does Hary-o mention that she had been taken 'to view an Exhibition of Young Ladies' talents which was very tedious'. And this, at a time when Queen Charlotte's long string of daughters were perpetually employed in those ornamental pastimes beloved by Mrs Delany and which had played such a part in Bulstrode life when Elizabeth Elstob was governess.

At Frogmore, Fanny Burney, herself, recorded: 'The walls of one room were painted by one Princess; all cabinets and tables of another were japanned by a second; carpets, stools and rugs were the work of a third.'

In their leisure hours, the Cavendish children played chess, read, or acted in family charades. Private theatricals were the rage and so were charitable works. Hary-o had a drawer in which she decided to keep 'all manner of clothes of different sorts for the poor people and when I hear of any in distress, I shall have my drawer ready'. Naturally, Selina encouraged all such inclinations for good works. In matters of dress, too, the Duchess was entirely original. She rarely wore powder in the morning and had made fashionable those long, flowing muslin dresses, those sky-blue sashes and simple garden straws which delight us in her exquisite portraits by Gainsborough and Sir Joshua Reynolds. Her children were equally simply dressed.

When the day came for Selina and her charges to leave England under Lady Spencer's capable wing, a small army of nursemaids, servants and couriers accompanied them. Delicate G and fat, healthy Hary-o were told not to drink water unless boiled and to clean their teeth and say their prayers every night on that dusty, uncomfortable, and slow drive through the dull countryside of Northern France. But once they reached Brussels, Selina's sermons were forgotten. There was darling Mama to kiss and fondle them again; to plan sudden, delicious treats; to indulge staid Selina's secret love for pretty clothes.

A fortnight before the expected birth of Georgiana's baby, the pressure of contemporary events forced the Duke and the Duchess to leave Brussels suddenly for France. Paris reached, a house was taken at Passy and her Grace hurried into it. It was not a moment too soon. Shortly after midnight of that same day, at one o'clock of the morning of 21st May 1790, the Marquis of Hartington was born.

'There never was a more welcome child,' wrote Ann Scafe, lady's maid to Lady Elizabeth Foster. A sentiment devoutly echoed through the entire Devonshire household.

But scarcely had the excitement died down when G, a sickly child, fell ill. Confined to her bed, her mother could do nothing for her. It was left to Lady Liz, Selina and Doctor Crofts, the family doctor, to fight for the child's life; through their combined efforts, little G survived. The Duchess could not thank Selina enough for having saved her beloved daughter. Before that tenderly expressed gratitude, Selina's last defences went down; her heart, single in its affection and steel-true, was made over, exclusively, to 'her dear children', and their mother, the Duchess. It became Devonshire property for life.

On their return to England, life resumed its normal course in the schoolroom. There were daily lessons, walks in Kensington Gardens, and carriage drives. There was another small pupil; shy and quiet Caroline St Jules, who shared G and Hary-o's lessons. Her French parentage was discreetly stressed and no one remarked openly on her odd likeness to the Duke and Lady Liz whose child she was.

In the summer of 1791, they were all at Bath where Selina met the well-known authoress, Miss Fanny Burney. 'Lady Spencer introduced me to Miss Trimmer, who is a pleasing but not pretty young woman, and seems born with her excellent mother's amiableness and serenity of mind.' (Monday, 1st September 1791)

Unfortunately, there came a distressing time now, for Selina and her charges. On 3rd November 1791, Georgiana, Duchess of Devonshire set sail from Southampton with her sister Lady Duncannon (afterwards Lady Bessborough), and their mother, Lady Spencer. She was to be away for nearly two years. A sequence of unhappy events culminating in the disaster that she was with child by Charles Grey, had led to this departure.

Hardly a day passed during her sad exile abroad when

Georgiana was not writing to her beloved children left far behind. Selina had it all her own way now that the angelic mother, whose infectious gaiety and impetuous plans had so richly coloured their dull schoolroom had vanished. The days came and went, monotonously, punctuated by polite but rather awed visits to their lethargic father, outstretched in his chair, a victim always to gout, while they waited, breathlessly, for those wonderful letters which came continuously from their mother. There were informative letters to help in the education of her dearest G or amusing letters, decorated by charming miniature sketches in water-colour or sepia, to interest Hary-o. Gay letters, sad letters, just as if their mother was speaking to them. They wrote back in their unformed, childish hands, supervised by Selina, telling darling Mama how Selina had organised an instructive visit to a Shawl Factory one day; another, taken them to look at Sir Ashton Lever's famous collection of Corals and Derbyshire spars. Clinging to every tiny scrap of news, precious as gold-dust, the Duchess replied how she, too, would collect mineral specimens for them on her travels. Now she sent a phosphorescent stone from Bologna; now a dried sprig of laurel from Virgil's tomb; now a pinch of cinders from Potyici. What were they reading with Selina, she asked? Was it still Rollin or the Iliad? Selina was always remembered and her love sent 'to Selina too – who tho' she is not my child is very dear to me from her kindness and care of my own Dear Brats'. (Nice, 8th April 1792)

Like a shaft of April sunlight striking down through a bank of cloud, came the news that the Duchess was on her way home. The Duke had consented at last to her return. For many days after her arrival, the excitement of her homecoming persisted and schoolroom law and order, so dear to Selina, was flung to the winds. At any moment of the day, the Duchess would appear to suggest this or that entrancing ploy to give her children pleasure. She even rose early to be more with them. What could Selina do? Like a dry, reluctant twig, she was caught up and carried along the sparkling stream of Madam's bubbling mood and gaiety. In dismay she saw her beloved routine which she had maintained so easily in Madam's absence, being put lightly on one side. It was so bad for her dear children, all these frivolous parties and outings. Querulously, Selina wrote off to Lady Spencer that she intended to speak her mind to the Duchess, telling her 'even harsh truths and where she errs in her treatment writing to her with a freedom and severity to which she is little used'. Full of stout, Trimmerian courage, she confided to the Dowager how 'she would tread the thorny path to duty and put a stop to much of the hurry and the dissipation that was to have taken place'. (7th April 1796)

But in reply to Selina's terse epistle to the Duchess, there came such a sweet little note sent by hand to her room, begging her forgiveness for her thoughtless behaviour, that Selina's heart melted completely. From that day, 'dear Madam' could do no wrong. Another victim had fallen to her famous charm.

The months flew by and they were at Chatsworth for the summer, dear Chatsworth, where Selina could retire to the peaceful security of her own room – the Upper Bow. Hart had been placed in her charge now. He was a proud, passionate and very obstinate little boy, who would argue with her for hours on end. But, like his sister, Hary-o, he had to give way to a stronger will than his own. Years later, he paid a charming tribute to the memory of his old governess in his *Handbook to Chatsworth*, describing: 'That smoky old place, our sitting-room, looking over the Court and seeing nothing but the smoky back of those busts, that now decorate the roof of the old greenhouse. There sat Selina – mild and good. Her greatest trial must have been the relations. To teach us was enough for mortal patience; but when the wildness next to the insanity of the clever but unfortunate Calantha (Caro Ponsonby) was added; I suppose a charm accompanied it, that enabled the instructress to endure such sallies found on her table as :

" The orange and the lemon pale
With Selly's cheek may vie ;
But ah ! no maid that is not frail
Has such a jet-black eye ! " '

Selina's hands were full, indeed, and her schoolroom over-crowded by new-comers.   There were Lady Liz's two Foster sons, serious plain Frederick and lively Augustus, and Augustus Clifford, two years older than Hart whom he resembled strongly. Caro Ponsonby who spent much time with her Cavendish cousins, benefited immensely from Selina's calm and comforting presence. At one time, Lady Bessborough had feared that her wild tantrums and hysteria might unhinge her brilliant but ill-balanced mind, permanently. But Selina had come to the rescue. She so organised Caro's life, seeing that she ate more digestible food and giving her *sal volatile* before an impending nerve-storm, that a wonderful improvement set in. When Selina suggested that the child should stay with her mother at Brentford for further treatment, Lady Bessborough consented gladly. Dear Selina! She always knew what to do for the best.   Her own children might call her '*Raison Sévère*' or '*Vent de Bise*' but it was only in fun. Knowing that she was their port and safest anchorage in any storm, they all took their troubles to her. They teased her, too, when they grew older with their silly school-girl chatter of a secret marriage between her and Mr Adair, a habitué of Devonshire House. Mrs Trimmer-Adair, they called her, which made Selina bridle and flush but which she adored all the same, being incurably romantic.

Caro Ponsonby has given her own description of this crowded and gay Whig schoolroom where 'they were served on gold in the morning and carried their own plates down at night and believed the world to be divided between Dukes and beggars. . . . We had no idea that bread and butter was made, how it came, we did not pause to think; but had no doubt that fine horses must be fed on beef. My kind Aunt Devonshire had taken me in when my mother's ill-health prevented my being at home.'

Besides the two Caros (Caro Ponsonby and Caro St Jules) there was Corisande de Grammont with her pretty French mouthings and shruggings; her liquid eyes. She was a great flirt and Selina had to keep careful watch on her.

Charades in which all her girls acted and mock concerts performed by 'Signorina Gina' and 'Signor Gugliemo' (Hart) and 'Signorinas Henrighetta & Carolina' were now the rage. Selina had learnt that where her aristocratic pupils were concerned, education was not solely a matter of serious book-learning. Graceful manners – how to walk and talk with ease and dignity – had to be acquired besides knowledge of history, languages and mathematics. Selina's own views broadened under the Duchess's gracious influence and she grew less Brentford-minded.

'Selina is always right and certainly could the world be new-formed and no impropriety suffered, how far happier it would be. Also it would be happier to lead a retired life. But your lot is cast in another line; and to do your duty and be an example to it, is my ardent wish.' So the sympathetic Duchess wrote to shy G when she was suffering pangs of adolescent piety and refused, point-blank, to attend the Opera. Her girls, Selina was told, need not play cards on a Sunday if they did not wish to. But music was permissible. Sunday, after all, was 'a chearful day' and her mother, Lady Spencer, had often 'had musick on Sunday evening'. They would follow this example at Devonshire House, declared Madam. Apart from such small differences there was peace and order in Selina's school-room even though Hary-o and Caro Ponsonby would run 'mad as March haires' all over the house and every day came sounds of incessant practising. One girl on the harp; another on the pianoforte; a third (it was Caro St Jules) on the guitar.

In 1800, Lady Georgiana Cavendish was presented at court and became engaged to young Lord Morpeth. Their marriage followed in March 1801.

A year later, in August 1802, Selina took her girls and Hart for a holiday to Ramsgate, lodging in the smaller of the

two houses, taken by the Duchess. It had an unattractive outlook, its small windows facing not the sea, but some dreary,
flat fields, marked by a solitary windmill. It was a long walk
to the pier and the weather was unbearably hot. Tempers ran
high, particularly Hart's. He hated his room and argued
angrily with Selina about it. Still, the bathing made up for
their cramped quarters although they had to dip themselves
decorously into the water, chaperoned by Selina, who had
been shocked by the way little Miss Talbot tossed her small
fat body about in the waves. Between four and six she took
her charges out on the pier or along the cliffs and they had
all to be in bed by half-past ten at the latest.

When Lady Bessborough joined her sister and brother-in-
law in the larger house, rented by the Duchess, she wrote to
Lord Granville Leveson-Gower, in a carping mood, telling
him: 'Ramsgate is a sad Idle place for our Children'. For
once in her life Selina no doubt agreed with Her Ladyship.

In the year that followed, Hary-o came out under her
mother's wing. Only Hart remained in the schoolroom, reading aloud to Selina; then he, too, left for Harrow. Sadly, Selina
put away her globes and her grammar books and departed on
a long visit to Lady Spencer at Holywell.

Faithfully, Hary-o continued writing to her 'Dearest Selina',
telling her how 'often in the most crowded assemblies your
idea comes to my mind and prevents many giddy and foolish
things I should otherwise do or say'. Her governess's influence was still far-reaching.

About this time, Miss Trimmer was asked by the Prince of
Wales whether she would accept the post of 'sub-preceptress'
to his only child, the lively Princess Charlotte. After some
hesitation, Selina tactfully declined the honour; even if her
own dear children had grown up, she still felt herself to be
part and parcel of the Devonshire family and wished to
be available when needed. As usual, she made the right
decision.

Early in March 1806, the Duchess went to Court, where

she caught cold and came home, shivering. She took to her bed and became seriously ill. After a prolonged and terrible struggle, fighting to overcome her only enemy, Death, the end came for Georgiana, Duchess of Devonshire, on 30th March.

At first, it was quite impossible for anyone to believe that her vital and adorable personality was no more. Every day people gathered to stare, long and silently, at the sombre hatchments displayed, on the low, brown façade of her London home while the whole of society mourned.

Hary-o Cavendish was left in an awkward position. By right, she was her father's hostess and should have controlled his household but Lady Liz remained glued to his side, giving her own orders and even plagueing poor Hary-o to go about with her, openly. Naturally, her grandmother and her sister, Lady Morpeth, objected strongly to this impossible state of affairs. On the other hand, Hary-o could not live apart from her father without giving rise to malicious talk. So Selina returned to Devonshire House as her official chaperone. Affectionately nicknamed 'La Fée Vigèle' by Hary-o, Selina was present at all family meals and rarely left her side. For several months, then, this odd quartette composed of Duke and daughter, titled mistress and prim governess lived at Devonshire House, gossiped over by all London.

It was not easy for either Hary-o or Selina to keep their tempers in the face of Lady Liz's continual visits to Hary-o's room where she lay suffering one severe Cavendish cold after another. Stiffly upright in a chair beside her bed, sat Selina, dosing her with sirrup of poppies and magnesia and generally keeping guard. As Hary-o told her grandmother: 'She (Lady Liz) is in one thing very tiresome to me; constant *controversies* with Miss Trimmer who really endeavours to keep out of them always talking to her on some religious subject and forcing her to say things that she may dispute them.' (19th November 1806)

Although Selina dearly loved an argument she put a strong

curb on her sharp tongue during this difficult time and remained silent. She had always disliked Lady Liz who, in turn,
said Selina affected her 'like the North East wind which in the
brightest sunshine has still some chill in it'.

In the summer of 1807, Hary-o departed on a long visit to
her sister at Castle Howard and Selina returned home. But
later in October, they were all four back in town with Lady
Liz trying, slyly, to get Harriet to accompany her to Brighton
for a month. In despair, Hary-o tells the Dowager of 'my
difficulties with regard to Lady Elizabeth (left as I am at her
mercy), for Miss Trimmer being with me does not in the least
prevent her persecuting me from morning till night'. (Devonshire House, Saturday, 31st October)

Although a plot was hatching for the Dowager to come
to her rescue, Hary-o had sudden qualms that between two
such strong-minded women as her indomitable grand-
parent and her resolute governess, something might be done
'ill-judged or violent that should put me in the most painful
and distressing situation', she told her sister. But as the
Dowager and Selina were past mistresses of social subterfuge,
life continued peaceably enough on the surface; what was
even more important, the Duke was excessively civil to *La
Fée Vigèle* who remained 'the greatest resource and comfort
to me', declared Hary-o.

À deux, then, they spent their mornings, reading or playing
chess, and in the afternoon calling on the Dowager. Meals
were sometimes awkward with Lady Liz enthusing over the
Duke's new litter of puppies that would play all over the
dining-room floor. ' "Oh, look! look! The dearest loves. The
sweetest t'ings!" she would cry while Miss T looks on in
maiden mediation fancy free with the courage not to conceal
how very much this interesting topic bores her', Hary-o wrote
to her sister. Ruthless, brave Selina.

During the winter and following spring, Harriet Cavendish
went out into Society under the wing of her aunt, Lady Bessborough, and it is winter again, the winter of 1808, before

Selina bobs up at Chiswick where Hary-o is staying, with good advice.

'Miss Trimmer came to me the day before yesterday. A dear woman, but as Doctors give some physic before some illness to prepare patients, she always gives me lectures, not upon any harm I have done in the past, but in case there should be any in the future, and like another Cassandra, predicts to me many sins that I may perhaps commit.'

But Hary-o was never irked by her governess's moralisings. On this occasion, she just laughed and took Selina off to London to see her grandmother. Spring came and while marriage plans quickened between Lady Liz and her father, Lord Granville Leveson-Gower, her aunt's long-established lover, began to pay court to her. Her grandmother, sister, and governess, all looked on, wondering if she would encourage the handsome young man whom she had known all her life, disliked, and nicknamed 'Doodle', once.

Surrounded by such a phalanx of celebrated relations, contemporary opinion must have criticised Harriet Cavendish's choice of a confidante in the odd situation in which she now found herself. But there are no ties so strong as those made in childhood. These only endure. Who knows us so well as our old nanny, over-fond though she may be? Who can better gauge our mental capacities and point to the goal in reach than our governess, equally fond but more critical? It was the most natural thing in the world for poor, perplexed Harriet Cavendish to turn to the one person she always called 'the dearest and best of friends'. Had not she been entrusted to Selina as a child by her mother and told to obey her implicitly? Perhaps, in the deserted garden at Chiswick, in those empty, pale rooms, with their delicately plastered walls and ceilings, that were still haunted by her mother's spirit, a silvery voice whispered to Hary-o, her puzzled daughter: 'Talk to Selina, my child. Follow her advice.'

To that rigid rock of decorum, then, Harriet Cavendish wrote almost daily. This was her governess's greatest hour.

She had helped her girls in many a love affair before now 'and never was anybody so pleased or so proud as she had been of that rôle. It gave her what is all I am afraid she must ever expect, the appearance of a flirtation. She makes mystery more mysterious and silence more silent,' Harriet had once written.

But now she heard that her dearest girl, for whom she wanted only the best in life, was being courted by the most eligible young man in Whig society. It was all as it should be but – ah, yes, there was a formidable *but*. There was Lady Bessborough, in fact, looming large as life and casting an ominous shadow across the path of her retreating lover.

In a letter, dated 8th October 1809, Hary-o Cavendish outlines her peculiar position to Selina for the first time.

'I was hurried yesterday, my dearest Selina, and had not time to say half I wished to do – Lady B acts in every way a most extraordinary part. We have every reason to believe (from confidence betrayed *de part et d'autre*) that she obtained a promise from Lord G. (Granville) before he joined us at B (Badminton). Ought I, dearest Selina, ever to think of a man over whom she has such claims or such influence as this? . . . You must let me see you as soon as I return, my dearest Selina. I cannot tell you what an incalculable blessing your friendship is to me and the consolation it is to be able to place the utmost confidence in you – I will not rely on myself – I will pray for the assistance I feel so much in need of and hope from it that peace, which I am sure the world cannot give. . . .

'God bless you, my best and dearest friend. Whatever fate may be, I can but keep myself steady in principle, act as you would approve, and make religion the great rule of my conduct, I cannot be very miserable. There is here so much to suffer and so little to enjoy that I am more convinced than ever of the folly and madness of those who live for this life alone. Help me to become worthy of a better and believe me – ever yrs, HARRIET CAVENDISH. Will you write me a few lines immediately, which will still find me here – the day of our departure is not settled.'

How Selina's heart must have warmed when she received this letter. Of course, the child could count on her advice and love. For who knew better than she that where Harriet Cavendish gave her hand, she would give her heart; that warm, generous heart at loggerheads so often with her shrewd and highly-principled Cavendish-Spencer mind? And then, no doubt, Selina sighed as she sat frowning, quill in hand, before replying to poor undecided Hary-o staying at Lord Cawdor's in South Wales. Somehow, Selina knew that her ex-pupil's affections were already engaged to the handsome young man of the almond-shaped 'occhi azzuri' with their long look.

Ten days later, Hary-o writes to Selina again; Selina, whom she is all impatient to see because 'I have so much to say that I am not at liberty to write', adding 'I pity Lady Bessborough from the bottom of my heart . . . I forgive her most sincerely for any artifices or duplicity in her conduct to me.'

Installed with the Dowager at Holywell, Selina could not go to Hary-o now at Chiswick. Dear Chiswick! where the moth-brown leaves of autumn floated down on the sodden lawns and the damp mists off the river added their chill to the chill of Hary-o's love-stricken heart. 'It is all I can do to keep up my spirits for the various difficulties I have to encounter at my return. But I have many comforts, many blessings – your kindness and friendship first in the list, my dearest, best of friends. Ever yrs, H. C. P s Read to yourself.'

Beside the fire flickering in the drawing-room at Holywell, Selina read and kept silent. But the die was suddenly cast and Hary-o made her momentous decision. On Tuesday, 14th November, Lord Granville Leveson-Gower proposed to and was accepted by Harriet Cavendish. She was never to regret the step taken by her that damp autumnal evening. For her marriage with 'adored Granville who would make a barren desert smile' was a very happy one.

As Christmas approached, Hary-o wrote to the only being

who had never failed her. She wrote from Chiswick, that dear
and lovely shell of so much vanished beauty.

'My Dearest Selina,

I send you the enclosed bracelet as a little remembrance
from me. On Sunday (24th December 1809) I shall have a
right to the initials I have had engraved upon it.

I do assure you, my dearest Selina, that at this most important and interesting moment I often think of your past
conduct to me, with affection and gratitude not to be expressed.

God bless you, my dearest friend,

Ever yrs most affectly,

HARRIET CAVENDISH'

What were Selina's thoughts as she clasped Hary-o's bracelet round her wrist? Did she realise that here was the visible
proof of how one governess had gained the respect and love
of her pupils by adhering always to what she thought was
right and best? Selina Trimmer has had her detractors. She
has been accused more than once of clinging to standards too
narrow for the brilliant social spheres in which she moved so
primly; of administering 'a little bitter always into one's cup'
as Hary-o had put it once, teasingly. But what had Georgiana
Devonshire wished her children to have most? Those same
high principles rigidly instilled by moralising Selina when they
were young and malleable to give them that stability of
character which she, their mother, had so sorrowfully lacked.

There is little more to add. After Hary-o's marriage Selina
divided her time between the Dowager Lady Spencer and
her own Brentford home where her sisters, Julia, Elizabeth
and Lydia, remained busily occupied in carrying on their
ageing mother's charitable works. On 5th December 1811,
Mrs Trimmer died quietly in her chair; so peaceful was her
end, so easily her active spirit called away, that when Selina

found her, she thought her dear mother's head was bowed in sleep, not death.

In 1814, old Lady Spencer passed away and Selina returned home for good. But whenever a Devonshire family crisis was pending, up she would bustle from Brentford to see her 'dear Children'. On the death of Lady Bessborough, abroad, she called with Hary-o at Cavendish Square on a visit of condolence. Harriet wrote to her sister: 'My last day was a *triste* one. I went with Miss Trimmer to C S and saw there Caroline, William, Duncannon, and William Ponsonby. . . . Caroline to whom I went with every feeling of interest and kindness awakened, contrived somehow or other, to deaden both.' (Wherstead, November 1821)

But Selina could be more sympathetic where poor Caro Lamb, her ex-pupil was concerned. When she lay seriously ill a year later and everyone was distracted by her state, Selina wrote to Hart, now her 'Dear Duke': 'Lady Caroline's poor wayward pitiable nature will always be a torment to herself and others as long as she lives.'

Yes, Selina knew. It was kind, thoughtful Hart, who had sent her a portrait of his beloved mother and one of himself to hang in her room. Critically biased as ever, Selina had declared that his picture did not do him justice. What portrait could have of her darling boy?

Characteristically, she added in this letter, 'I am difficult to please,' and then concluded: 'I will not take up your time with my idle nonsense and may the choicest of Heaven's blessing attend you where and whatever you do.' (13th December 1826)

Her health was failing and she had taken to her wing-chair. With her beloved Devonshire portraits to look at and Hary-o's bracelet on her wrist, she attended to her voluminous correspondence. Another generation was growing up, a new tribe of little Howards and Leveson-Gowers. Hart who 'struggled with a sad and solitary soul' remained a bachelor. He was the most eligible *parti* in the United Kingdom with every match-making mother after him. Yes, there were always fresh interests for Selina. There were memories too: unique and very precious . . .

That historic winter – was it 1802? – when they nearly all froze to death at Chatsworth. What fun it had been, those out-of-door games organised by 'dear Madam', who had ordered the estate carpenter to make special little wooden sledges and go-carts. The Storm that had followed and then the Big Fire. She could still hear Caro Ponsonby's shrieks as the gallery window blew in on her as she was passing. She had picked her up from under the muffling curtains and shattered glass, thinking the child's hysterical screams would never stop. But she had calmed her, finally. Ramsgate! Those gusty walks along the pier with the Lamb boys whom she disliked as much as their mother, Lady Melbourne, always hovering near. *'Un agneau de plus*, Selina.' Hary-o had cried to tease her. And then, silly child, she had giggled.

But it was Madam, 'dear Madam', with her soft drawling voice and sweet smile, who dominated Selina's world of unique memories; Madam's the ghost which kept faithful tryst in that shadowy dream-world where they visited together an empty schoolroom to see the dust lying thick on Hary-o's harp and the books of childhood put away forever.

During the winter of 1828, Selina suffered a severe illness and her last letter, dated 4th December 1828, is addressed to the Duke. Optimistic as ever, she declared her health improved though 'her whole nervous system shaken by the remedies used'. Selina had always enjoyed doctoring others but she heartily disliked being a patient herself. Feeling the end of her long life is near, she adds: 'Adieu, my dearest Duke, may every blessing attend you. Yrs most gratefully and affectionately, S. Trimmer.'

There is one more letter dictated by her, which stresses again her love and gratitude for the youngest of her three long-loved Cavendish children. Selina's last thoughts were for Hart, left deaf and solitary among his great possessions.

On 31st January 1829, Julia Trimmer informed William Spencer, sixth and last (of his line) Duke of Devonshire, of the death 'of that dear individual who loved you with an affection quite maternal. I believe,' Julia continued, 'that she enjoyed during her life as much happiness as falls to the lot of any in this world.'

What better epitaph could anyone wish for? Selina had passed her life among the great and thus known greatness herself. She, whom Hary-o had laughingly declared to be 'the Arch advocate of Reason' had taught her children much, but they, in turn, had enlarged and softened her restricted Trimmer mind. Though they had teased her, they had loved her too.

Among the family governesses of the eighteenth century – that period of fine manners and fine taste – Selina Trimmer is unique. Unique for the position of trust she held at Devonshire House, where 'she was treated in every respect like one of the young lady Cavendishes', and never once heard her adored mistress say, 'Silver forks for the young ladies, a steel one for the Governess', like poor Miss Latetia Grey.

Selina is buried in the Trimmer vault at Ealing Parish Church but I like to think of her still inhabiting the room which she made so much her own; that smoky old place, the Upper Bow, transformed today into an ordinary, white-painted bedroom which lies at the end of a long corridor at Chatsworth. There sits *La Fée Vigèle*, the guardian of a schoolroom which has vanished forever. She is a ghost, as faithful and devoted in death, as she was in life to the great family she served, while outside the sun shines down upon that exquisite Derbyshire valley, upon that great square pile of a golden house, empty and deserted, too – Chatsworth.

CHAPTER FOUR

The Regency Governess

'Fortitude is a necessary virtue in all – in a governess as indispensable
as talent, temper, patience, principle, politeness, meekness and modesty.'
The Private Governess, 1826

In 1814, Lady Sydney Morgan published her period romance,
O'Donnell, in which a governess was featured for the first
time as a romantic heroine. This was the sullen and silent
Miss O'Halloran, who became the lovely, laughing Duchess
of Belmont, a brilliant wit and ravisher of hearts. From her,
there descended a whole race of glamour-governesses in nineteenth century fiction.

Two years after the publication of *O'Donnell*, Jane Austen
produced in *Emma* (1816) the perfect portrait of the beloved
governess and family friend in an oval Regency frame. She
was Miss Taylor, better known by her married name of Mrs
Weston, in whose admirable care Emma Woodhouse grew
up.

'There was not a creature in the world to whom she spoke
(Emma) with such unreserve . . . half an hour's uninter-
rupted communication of all those daily matters which daily
private happiness depends on was one of the first gratifica-
tions of each . . . the very sight of Mrs Weston, her smile, her
touch, her voice, was grateful to Emma.'

Except for a brief spell at the Abbey School, Reading, Jane
Austen was educated entirely at home by her parents. She
never had a governess. But carefully observed details concerning the Regency governess appear in her novels as nearly
every Hampshire county family of her acquaintance could
provide her with working models. Chief among them was
Miss Sharpe, governess at Godmersham Park, Kent, to

the little Knight girls, Fanny, Lizzie, and Marianne, whose father was Jane's brother.

Some people thought Miss Sharpe 'a good-humoured, affectionate creature, but rather gushing and plaintive; she was not very quick or clever and her pupils were inclined to make fun of her'. But Aunt Jane took an immediate liking to her and after their first meeting in the summer of 1805, she sent this message to her through Cassandra Austen, her sister.

'Pray say everything kind for us to Miss Sharpe, who could not regret the shortness of our meeting in Canterbury more than we did. I hope she returned to Godmersham as much pleased with Mrs Knight's beauty and Miss Milles' judicious remarks as those ladies respectively were with hers.' (Goodnestone Farm, Friday, 30th August)

At Godmersham, Aunt Jane usually occupied the Yellow Room and was in and out of Miss Sharpe's schoolroom. She often volunteered to hear 'the little girls Read', and declared that she never found 'much to try the patience or hurt the spirit at Godmersham'. As *Mansfield Park* is the literary mirror of what life must have been like at Godmersham, Ann Sharpe might well be the prototype of Miss Lee, who taught the Miss Bertrams how to put the map of Europe together, to sew and embroider, and to wonder later at the ignorance of gentle Fanny Price, their cousin.

On Miss Sharpe's departure from Godmersham, Jane Austen corresponded with her warmly and was soon pressing her to come and stay at Chawton Cottage. She felt that Miss Sharpe 'is born, poor thing, to struggle with Evil'. But this visit never materialised for different reasons. The very fact, though, that a visit was planned shows the friendly footing they were on. Like Selina Trimmer, Ann Sharpe was treated as one of the family at Godmersham.

After the death of lovely Mrs Knight in 1808 Miss Sharpe was succeeded by a Miss Clewes, who seemed 'the very governess they have been looking for these ten years – longer

Richmal Mangnall, from a portrait by John Downman

The Regency Governess

coming than J. Bond's last shock of corn. If she will only keep good and amiable and perfect! Clewes is better than Clowes and is it not a name for Edward to pun on? is not a clew a nail?' (Chawton, Tuesday, 9th February 1813)

All this from Jane to Cassandra, of course.

On the 23rd June 1814, the post brought a letter from Miss Sharpe to Jane Austen. After a depressing period, she seemed to be in a comparative state of comfort and Cassandra was informed by her sister, that Ann was 'at Sir W. P's in Yorkshire, with the children, and there is no appearance of her quitting them. Of course, we lose the pleasure of seeing her. She writes highly of Sir Wm I do so want him to marry her. There is a Dow. Lady P presiding there to make it all right . . . Oh, Sir Wm! Sir Wm! how I will love you if you love Miss Sharpe!'

But in spite of this delicious promise, Sir William Pilkington did not marry Miss Sharpe. It remained for Miss Austen, now a famous authoress, to write one of her last letters to her governess friend on the eve of her departure for Winchester. She was a sick woman, having been in bed over a month 'with only removals to a Sopha', her dearest Ann was told. 'Wherever Distress falls you are expected to supply Comfort. Ly P— writing to you even from Paris for advice – It is the influence of Strength over weakness indeed! *Sick* or *well*, Jane Austen signed herself: '*ever yr attached friend.*' Barely a month later she was dead.

Ann Sharpe never married and ended her career by keeping a Young Ladies' Establishment in Liverpool. Similar schools were opening everywhere in Regency England. Outside many a Gothic villa in the country, a blue signboard was seen. On it was painted in big gold letters: YOUNG LADIES BOARDED AND EDUCATED.

In spite of this new and often pretentious kind of parlour-board education, criticised severely by Jane Austen in *Emma*, young females were no better informed. According to Hannah More, there were still too many 'superficial wives and incompetent and illiterate governesses being brought up on short cuts to Knowledge'.

Girls now studied literature in 'selections' specially edited so as not to bring a blush to their cheeks. Lessons were invariably conducted in the form of *Question* and *Answer*, in the Regency schoolroom; the governess putting the question to her pupil who had learnt the correct reply, parrot-like. As Elizabeth Grant recorded in her *Memoirs of a Highland Lady*, 'No explanations were either asked or given, so the brain was by no means over-excited, and the writing and cyphering and pianoforte lessons which followed the drier studies of the morning pleased me exceedingly'. Incidentally, Eliza Grant and her sister, a lively crew, had several governesses before a little fat dumpling of a woman (these words are her own) called Miss Elphick took up her position firmly in the Rothiemurchus schoolroom and remained there for seven years.

Well-educated women like Miss Hannah More and Miss Maria Edgeworth objected to the method of cheating children into learning 'by Abridgements, Beauties and Compendiums' and openly said so. A very special place was given to 'the Use of the Globes' in the Regency schoolroom. It was considered particularly suited for Young Ladies, as opposed to Young Persons and no well-bred girl's education was complete without a full knowledge of the mysteries of the Globes, Celestial and Terrestial.

Unlike the schoolroom of the eighteenth century, the Regency schoolroom was in a remote part of the house. Sophia, Caroline and Jane, leading a cloistral life, upstairs, with their governess, were in a world quite apart from Charlotte, Amelia and Marianne, seeking husbands in the drawing-room downstairs, with Mamma. Miss Crawford put the whole question of a young lady being 'out' or 'not out' in a nutshell to Fanny Price in *Mansfield Park*.

'The distinction is so broad. Manners as well as appearance are generally so different. A girl not out has always the same dress – a close bonnet, for instance – looks very demure and never says a word.'

With her pupils, the Regency governess put on that same close bonnet and assumed the same demure air till gradually she was transformed into that dull, brown, resigned creature whom Mrs Vincy described in *Middlemarch* as 'just the sort of person for a governess' and her daughter Rosamund dismissed as 'uninteresting and not young'.

From the year *Mansfield Park* was published in 1815, it may be said that the well-bred girl was banished with her governess, to some dreary upper room till her older sister's marriage allowed her to come out. Only then could she be petted and noticed by visitors; only then could she be included in the family invitations to local assembly balls. Lady Catherine de Bourgh, a great stickler for etiquette, was shocked that all the Bennett girls were 'out' together and that no resident governess graced the Longburn household. (*Pride and Prejudice*)

Employing the services of a governess had been *sine qua non* in upper-class English families since Tudor days; in Regency times, the practice was adopted by prosperous middle-class parents but with what a difference of approach to the poor creature in their employ.

Ellen Weeton 1776-18—

Knowing only undiluted sorrow in her long grey life, Ellen Weeton, with her haggard face and gaunt body, might well have sat for the portrait of that pale melancholy governess recommended by St Jerome to Lady Laeta. Even Ellen's home-background, the rugged and stern landscape of the Lake District with its bare fells and small market towns built of harsh grey stone, that harboured the first labour troubles, are as much part of her lonely life as the splendid pomps and ceremonies of Chatsworth and Devonshire House were part of Selina Trimmer's.

There is an earlier governess with whom Ellen Weeton has some affinity. Like Elizabeth Elstob, Ellen yearned from childhood to acquire knowledge: 'Oh! how I have burned to learn Latin, French, the Arts, the sciences, anything rather than the jog-trot way of sewing, teaching, writing copies and washing dishes every day. Of my Arithmetic I was very fond and advanced rapidly. Mensuration was quite delightful, Fractions, Decimals, etc . . .'

But Ellen was unfortunate in having a detestable brother called Tom. Instead of helping her to learning, like William Elstob had helped his Elizabeth, Tom made Ellen deny herself everything but the bare necessities of life, first to give him an education superior to hers; secondly, to set him up in the legal profession. No wonder that she cried out in despair, one day: 'Why are not females permitted to study physic, divinity, astronomy, etc, etc, with their attendent chemistry, botany, logic, mathematics, etc? To be sure the mere study is not prohibited, but the practice is, in a measure. Who would employ a female physician, who would listen to a female divine, except to ridicule? I could laugh myself almost at the idea.'

Poor Ellen! she would not laugh today. But there was a long time to go before the narrow-minded Tom Weetons of this world would accept the distinguished figure of Doctor Maud Royden in the pulpit, or tolerate the plate of a female specialist set up with theirs in Harley Street.

Ellen Weeton, the daughter of a slave-ship captain, was born on Christmas Day, 1776. On the death of her father five years later, her mother took her and her little brother, Tom, to live in the tiny hamlet of Upholland, four miles to the west of Wigan. Here Mrs Weeton opened a small day-school.

Ellen was her right hand, teaching and minding the young ones. In her spare time, though, she was always at her books or scribbling down the rhymes and verses that came to her as easily. Her mother, proud at first of her daughter's curious faculty for book-learning and versifying, later took fright.

She had no wish that Ellen, so useful as a kindergarten teacher should be taken for a poetess in embryo or even a local blue-stocking. So poor Ellen found herself discouraged on every possible occasion from pursuing her literary studies.

Hers was a hard girlhood. Besides teaching nine hours a day, she had to cook, sew and clean their home. When her mother suffered from severe asthma – as she did continually – Ellen contrived to do both their work. At the age of fourteen, Tom Weeton was articled to a solicitor in Preston, and mother and daughter pinched and scraped still further to pay his fees. They never saw fresh butter, sugar, pastry, meat, or cream; a lowering diet of bread and potatoes was their only fare. This lack of nourishing food and the confined life she led as a household drudge and kindergarten teacher came to affect Ellen, the growing girl, very seriously. For three years her health was in a precarious state; then, as she was recovering, her mother died, leaving her, not yet twenty-one, with the heavy burden of running their little school alone.

A ghastly time followed for poor Ellen trying to make two impossible ends meet. The dual effort to teach and to mind her scholars single-handed – she could not afford any assistance as what private income she derived from a small family estate in Sunderland was given over to her spoilt, ungrateful brother – proved too much. She lived amongst her pupils, a gaunt and desperately sick young woman. Sometimes, there was not a penny in the house with which to buy herself even a tiny roll for breakfast.

Early in the spring of 1808, Ellen determined to give up the unequal struggle at Upholland and try to secure an easier post in less remote surroundings. 'From being so much alone, I am now unfitted for society,' she confided to her unfeeling brother.

To give him his due, Thomas Weeton did try to find his sister more congenial work. In her name he applied for a vacancy as governess in Miss Richmal Mangnall's famous

Academy for Girls at Crofton, near Wakefield. But his application was refused. The great Miss Mangnall, whose *Historical Questions and Answers* had become a best seller in teaching circles, had been suited elsewhere. She was never to meet Miss Weeton.

When Ellen left Upholland, she took an unsuccessful holiday with brother Tom and his termagant wife, and then went as guest-companion to her sour friend, Miss Chorley. This visit was no more successful. Thrown back upon herself, as usual, solitary and sad, Ellen took lodgings in the remote little river-inn of Beacon's Gutter on Merseyside. Here, with the water lapping up to its door, Ellen was happy among the rough but kindly fishing folk, as Elizabeth Elstob had once been happy living among Evesham's asparagus growers. But misfortune suddenly came in the shape of two new lodgers: a raffish gentleman and his girl-friend, who had lately been his serving wench. With their rude behaviour and lavish tipping, this fine couple ruined the up till now peaceful and modest life at Beacon's Gutter for poor Ellen. She was forced to find rooms elsewhere. So she went to Liverpool to lodge with the kind Winkleys. In Ann Winkley, she soon found the sympathetic friend to whom her confidential letters are written.

In December, 1809, Ellen told Tom that she had answered the following advertisement brought to her notice by Mrs Winkley.

Wanted, in the neighbourhood of Kendal, a GOVERNESS *to superintend the Education of a young Lady. None need apply but such as can give good references as to ability and character. Apply to J. Gore.*

Ellen's application brought about an interview with an elderly gentleman called Barton, appointed by a Mr Pedder of Dove's Nest, Ambleside, to engage him a governess for his small daughter, who was to act as companion to his wife as well. Mr Barton asked Ellen what salary she wanted. 'I answered, "Thirty guineas". He engaged me, and I am going.'

So much for Ellen's boldness. She had procured a far

higher salary than it was customary to pay and double the one Charlotte Brontë received thirty years later.

On her arrival at Dove's Nest, a late eighteenth century house built under Wansfell, and with a pretty park sloping down to Lake Windermere, Ellen discovered that Mrs Pedder was a mere girl of seventeen, who had lately been employed as dairymaid at Mr Pedder's other home, Darwen Bank, near Preston. She was his second wife. Miss Pedder, aged ten, his only child by his first marriage, was subject to fits. She could have as many as five a day and her poor governess was expected to hold her down during each one. Although tolerably happy at Dove's Nest where there were physical comforts to enjoy like good food and warm fires, a genuine *cri de coeur* goes up in her Journal. 'The vexations that occur sometimes during the hours of instruction with a child of such strange temper would almost induce me to give up my present situation.' (20th January 1810)

A terrible tragedy occurred now. Little Miss Pedder set her clothes alight while standing too close to the fire. Miss Weeton alone kept her head and after beating the flames out, swathed her pupil's body round in bands of oiled linen till she looked like a small Egyptian mummy. But early the following morning, as she knelt praying beside the now ice-cold, unconscious little body, Ellen realised the child was dying and called Mr and Mrs Pedder. Shortly before 6 am Margaret Gertrude breathed her last.

Miss Weeton stayed on as companion to the young dairymaid wife although much wounded by Mr Pedder, who kept hinting that if his daughter had been watched more carefully the accident would never have happened. Was this her reward for having kept her head in such a crisis? From now on, she did more and more household sewing, ordered the meals, and coped with all staff problems. She continued pouring her heart out to Ann Winkley, telling her that life was really becoming too difficult as Mr Pedder when drunk was 'a vile despot' and when sober 'not many degrees removed from a complete fool'.

Mr Saul, a clergyman, came to stay with the Pedders. Miss Weeton was immediately attracted, but 'the great difference between a governess and a clergyman of family and fortune made me cautious of being in his company more than I could help, lest my heart should be involuntarily forming an attachment that might cause me years of unhappiness'.

There follows in the same letter a charming picture of Ellen seated on a grassy knoll just above Dove's Nest, playing happily on her flageolet. It is an exquisite warm day and Mr Green, the Lakeland painter, has asked her to stand godmother to his baby daughter. But misfortune in guise of Mr Saul is on its way. Ellen's gaiety at once leaves her for she feels 'too humble, too insignificant, too ignorant, and too poor to excite any attention from him'.

Although a clergyman had long been considered the right person for a governess to marry in polite circles, no governess was quite so humble-minded as poor Ellen Weeton. It seemed impossible for her to visualise even the beginning of a love affair; let alone stage the happy sequel to it.

So she struggled on through the severe Lakeland winter, stemming down that natural yearning of hers for the love of a good man which most governesses have felt, forced to participate in family life never wholly theirs.

In the early spring of 1811, Ellen could battle no more against her normal desire to be beloved and decided to free herself, once and for all, from the pain of meeting Mr Saul, again. Off she went, in her grey sarsenet bonnet and shabby mantle worked in black chenille, very much the same gaunt female that had arrived, two years before, to be governess to Margaret Gertrude. And Mrs Pedder, ex-dairymaid, was the only creature who sincerely mourned her departure from Dove's Nest.

In July 1812, Ellen became governess to the children of Mr Joseph Armitage, a rich manufacturer living at High Royd House, four miles from Huddersfield. A few months before, the North and South Ridings of Yorkshire had seen the Lud-

88

dite risings and Mr Armitage had been singled out for attention from a band of rioters. They had thrown stones at the windows of his home, Lockwood House, an incident which Charlotte Brontë made use of in her novel, *Shirley*. Because of this attack, Joseph Armitage had removed his wife and family to High Royd House near the little weaving village of Honley.

The Armitages, a young couple, gave Miss Weeton complete authority to do as she thought best for her charges. Like the little Inghams to whom Anne Brontë was a governess in the same district, years later, the little Armitages 'though well-ordered by their parents, when out of sight are as unruly, noisy, insolent, quarrelsome and ill-tempered, etc, as I ever met with'.

Ellen was in for a bad time and described how 'My time is totally taken up with the children; from 7 o'clock in the morning till half past 7, or 8 at night. I cannot lie longer than 6 o'clock in a morning; and, if I have anything to do for myself, in sewing, writing, and etc, I must rise sooner. At 7, I go into the nursery to hear the children say their prayers, and to remain with them till after they have breakfasted, when I go out with them whilst they play; and am often so cold that I join in their sports to keep warm myself. About half past 8, I breakfast with Mr and Mrs Armitage, and then return again to the children till 9, when we go into the schoolroom till 12. We then bustle on our bonnets, etc, for play or for a short walk. At one, we bustle them off again, to dress for dinner, to which we all sit down at quarter past; the children always dine with their parents. By the time dinner is well over, it is 2 o'clock, when we go in to school, and remain till 5.

'Whilst I am at tea in the parlour, the children eat their suppers in the nursery. I then go with them till 7, either walking out of doors, or playing within, as the weather may permit. I then hear their prayers and see them washed; at half past 7 they are generally in bed.'

Everywhere she went in the North, Ellen met with that growing, middle-class disdain of the governess, unknown to Selina Trimmer. Though Ellen declared that Mr and Mrs Armitage were pleasant enough with her, 'A governess is almost shut out of society; not choosing to associate with the servants, and not being treated as an equal by the heads of the house or their visitors, she must possess some fortitude and strength of mind to render herself tranquil or happy; but indeed, the master and mistress of a house, if they have any goodness of heart, would take pains to prevent her feeling her inferiority. For my own part, I have no cause of just complaint; but I know some that are treated in a most mortifying manner.'

Besides the possession of fortitude Miss Weeton stressed the importance of French in the equipment of a first-class governess. If only she had been taught French, 'I could have had a situation where I would have received a salary of a hundred pounds a year, in a family of distinction'. But Mrs Weeton had dismissed French as 'a very useless acquisition to the generality of English women!' Her daughter, Ellen, had suffered in consequence.

An interesting comment on everyday habits in different social spheres is recorded by Ellen when she watched, with horror, seven-year-old Sarah Ann Armitage being washed naked in the nursery. Evidently this was not done in her circles.

On the whole, though, she was happy at High Royd House where household matters were conducted with tradesman-like regularity. There was no lounging about after meals, no quarrelling, and no drunkenness as there had been at Dove's Nest. One day, Ellen went to supper with old Mrs Armitage who gave her a red dress. Ellen wrote how she looked *glowing* in it. She was fortunate. Some years later a governess would never have been allowed to wear red.

Of contemporary happenings like the Luddite terrors, Ellen makes no mention in her Journal. She is only concerned with the complete indifference of the Armitage parents to their children's education. Mr Armitage did not mind paying the governess her salary but he saw no reason why he should spend more of his money on equipping her schoolroom. When Ellen asked for some new books, she was told curtly that she could not have them. Eventually, though, she got her way and some were ordered from London. The Armitages did not take newspapers and were frankly non-intellectual. For Ellen, 'My own ideas must entertain me. I read very seldom; having, in the first place, but very little time for it, my own sewing and letter-writing occupying most of my leisure; and in the second place Mr & Mrs A having never offered to lend me any books except an Encyclopaedia, which is not an everyday kind of reading.'

Mrs Armitage was always 'expecting' and the house being prepared for an *accouchement*.

In the summer of 1813, while Ellen was taking a holiday at Liverpool she was asked by a Mrs Wade of Pot-Echee, near Douglas, Isle of Man, to go as her governess. Though Ellen's demand of a salary of £50 per annum was accepted, she decided to remain with the Armitages and passed the job on to her cousin.

Alas! Mrs Armitage begins 'expecting' again and grows odd-tempered. According to Ellen, she is Argus-eyed, stingy, and suspicious. The sky darkens familiarly for her and clouds gather. Five of the children develop whooping-cough, and the two worst sufferers are put to sleep with her. She gets no rest. No wonder, she gives notice. But when the day comes for her departure, she is all tears and so are the children. They cannot bear their dear 'Ugly face', as they called her, to go. They all get up at five in the morning and walk five miles with her, to mop their eyes and wave their hands, as she rattles off by stage-coach to Liverpool.

So ended Miss Weeton's life as a governess. For soon, she is to meet, and marry, the horrible Mr Aaron Stock, by whom she and their only child, a daughter called Mary, were so tragically misused. But that is another story. We are only concerned with Ellen as a Regency governess and the unique Journal she kept as such.

Her book was to await discovery for well over a century before being published in two volumes by the Oxford University Press in 1936, with a full and interesting introduction by her Editor, Mr Edward Hall.

Like Charlotte Brontë who followed in her footsteps as governess and endured the same kind of hardships, Ellen protested in her Journal – as Charlotte in her novels – at the way women of intellect were treated by people of inferior education and manners. Like Charlotte, too, Ellen suffered the misery of a mind aching for the relief of authorship; the sense of genius frustrated by her calling. Unlike Charlotte, Ellen Weeton never tasted the sweets of literary fame or knew how her Journal and Letters when published would receive instant recognition. Craving for the love and companionship continually denied during her long, tragic life, the figure of Ellen Weeton, Governess, stalks through the domestic Regency scene more like a gaunt spectre than a live woman.

CHAPTER FIVE

Triumvirate of Governesses

'A governess's experience is frequently, indeed, bitter, but its results are precious ; the mind, feeling, temper are there subjected to a discipline equally painful and priceless. I have known many who were unhappy as governesses, but not one who regretted having undergone the ordeal, and scarcely one whose character was not improved.'

CHARLOTTE BRONTË *to Mr Williams* (Haworth, 11th June 1848)

When Mrs Gaskell was asked to write Charlotte Brontë's biography, she revisited every scene connected with the main incidents of her life except those connected with what she called 'the two little pieces of private governess-ship'.

But if it had not been for these, Charlotte's heroine, poor plain and disconnected Jane Eyre, who was destined to revive the drooping spirits of hundreds of Early Victorian governesses, would not have been created. Put a governess anywhere near Charlotte during her life and she forsook the most brilliant company to speak to that socially ignored figure. Long after she had finished with being a governess she told Mrs Gaskell that: 'If I had to earn my living I would go out again, much as I dislike the life; for I think one should write out of the fullness of one's heart, spontaneously.'

Charlotte Brontë knew from what galling ingredients her heart's fullness had been compounded and that her particular genius had benefited from being a governess.

'The only glimpses of society I have ever had were obtained in my vocation of governess, and some of the most miserable moments I can recall were passed in drawing-rooms full of strange faces. At such times, my animal spirits would ebb gradually till they sank quite away; and when I could endure the sense of exhaustion and solitude no more, I used to steal off, too glad to find any corner where I could be

93

really alone. Still I know very well that though that experiment of seeing the world might give acute pain for the time, it would do good afterward.'

An over-sensitive, under-sized, touchy young girl, Charlotte was far less suited in temperament to be a governess than either Emily or Anne. But as the genteelly brought up daughter of a poor North Country parson, no other kind of profession was open to her. Since childhood, she confessed to Ellen Nussey, her life-long friend and confidante, she had felt 'the deep responsibility upon her; that she was an object of expense to those at home, and she must use every moment to attain the purpose for which she had been sent to school, *ie*, to fit herself for governess-life.'

This life began when she accepted kind Miss Wooler's offer to return as pupil-teacher to her old school, with Emily accompanying her as a boarder at reduced fees. It was a welcome reprieve for shy, gauche Charlotte to begin teaching under the affectionate eye of Miss Wooler. But it was in the familiar classroom at Roe Head that Charlotte learnt to loathe the profession that the social convention of her day forced her to adopt. It was her personal tragedy that she found no joy in teaching the young like the Saxon Lady, though we have Mary Taylor's assurance of 'how interesting Charlotte always made poetry and drawing to me'.

Try as hard as she could, Charlotte Brontë could not stifle the creative urge within her to write. In a letter to Robert Southey, written while she was at Miss Wooler's, she confessed how:

'I carefully avoid any appearance of pre-occupation and eccentricity, which might lead those I live among to suspect the nature of my pursuit . . . I have endeavoured not only attentively to observe all the duties a woman ought to fulfil, but to feel deeply interested in them. I don't always succeed, for sometimes when I am teaching or sewing I would rather be reading or writing; but I try to deny myself.' (16th March 1838)

In another letter to Ellen Nussey: 'If you knew my thoughts; the dreams that absorb me; and the fiery imagination that at times eats me up and makes me feel Society, as it is, wretchedly insipid you would pity me – I dare say despise me.' (10th May 1836) Here the kind and clever, elder sister who acted as self-appointed governess to Emily and Anne is not speaking but the paid teacher.

One afternoon, after Charlotte had finished correcting some of her pupils' work, she gave way to the poet and wrote *The Teacher's Monologue*.

> ' The room is quiet, thoughts alone
> People its mute tranquillity ;
> The yoke put off, the long task done,
> I am, as it is bliss to be,
> Still and untroubled. Now I see,
> For the first time, how soft the day
> O'er waveless water, stirless tree,
> Silent and sunny, wings its way . . . '

It speaks highly for Charlotte's powers of literary self-control that *The Teacher's Monologue* is her one and only governess-poem. While working for Miss Wooler, her health failed and she was forced to return home. Several months passed before she set out again in the summer of 1839 to be governess to Mrs Sidgwick of Stonegappe in Yorkshire.

The picture of Charlotte being inundated by oceans of sewing in her first private situation, being stoned at by one little Sidgwick and told by another, 'I love 'ou, Miss Brontë,' much to his mother's disgust, is familiar to many of us. The drawing-room at Swarcliffe where she sat, ignored by Mrs Sidgwick's friends, who were 'proud as peacocks' is not so far removed, either, from the one in which Jane Eyre sat listening to haughty Miss Blanche Ingram while she dismissed the whole race of governesses as mere *incubi*. Every governess-experience of Charlotte's was doomed to failure. Knowing little French – the ace-language still in a first-class governess's qualifications – unable to teach music and coming from a remote North Country parsonage, bare of noble patrons, Charlotte Brontë could not undertake the education of well-bred girls. Not for her the warm affections of a duchess that fortunate Selina Trimmer found at Devonshire House. Charlotte was equipped only to teach young children and to be a governess among the rich manufacturing families of the North where her profession was being looked down on more and more. This was her great misfortune.

By July 1839 she was back at Haworth, trying to forget the hateful Sidgwicks. But early in the New Year, she was corresponding with a Mrs Thomas Brooke, of Huddersfield, with a view to going out again as her governess. Unfortunately, there were no personal interviews for young governesses in those far-off days of difficult communication. Advertisements in the press were answered by letter, very formal letters, too, that offered no clues as to the kind of girl who was applying for a governess-post or the kind of mistress who might engage her. For the Brontë girls living in their remote moorland parish, the transport question was an expensive item which they had to consider carefully, before embarking on any journey. Mr Brontë was curiously unwilling to help in any travelling arrangement or have his daughters met when they arrived at Bradford. In consequence Charlotte and Anne knew little about the families that they were going to and their employers were equally in the dark about them.

As Mrs Brooke of Huddersfield wanted a governess who could teach music and singing, negotiations broke down between her and Charlotte. It was not until March of 1841 that Charlotte went to Mrs White, the jolly daughter of an exciseman, who lived at Upperwood House, Rawdon, six miles from Bradford.

The Whites of Upperwood were distinctly *nouveaux riches* but treated Miss Brontë respectfully as the daughter of a dignified member of the church. At least, the sewing did not assume the vast proportions it had at Stonegappe and the

The Governess, or The Poor Teacher, detail of a picture
by Richard Redgrave, RA

The Trimmer Villa in Windmill Lane, Brentford

The Palace of San Cristovao, a sketch by Maria Graham

little Whites were not 'the riotous little fiends' the Sidgwick children had been.

But the day came when Charlotte gave notice on the plea that she was going to Brussels to improve her French. When the final moment for parting arrived, she could write like Ellen Weeton in all truthfulness how it effaced 'the memory of much that had annoyed me while I was there, but, indeed, during the whole of the last six months they only made too much of me. I did not deserve it.'

Charlotte sent a book to one of the little Whites after she had left. Its fly-leaf has been preserved, on which is written: 'Sarah Louisa White, from her friend, C. Brontë, July 20 1841'.

Perhaps Miss Brontë the governess was not so indifferent to children, after all.

Eight months after the triumphant publication of *Jane Eyre* in 1847, Mr William Smith Williams, reader to Charlotte's publishers, sought her advice on a delicate family problem. Should his two daughters go out as governesses? The letters that Charlotte wrote in reply contain all that she thought and felt about the difficulties of being a governess. Written without rancour by a mature woman, they are a complete contrast to those written by her when, a touchy girl, she brooded over the imagined slights and insults offered to those in her profession.

Charlotte stressed to Mr Williams the supreme importance of the faculty which she thought she had lacked. This was 'the faculty not merely of acquiring knowledge but of imparting knowledge – the power of influencing young minds – that natural fondness for, that innate sympathy with, children.' Charlotte added that 'if this faculty is missing, the life of a teacher will be a struggle from beginning to end . . . she will have a wearing, wasting existence.'

She did not believe in the higher education for girls who wished to be governesses which was being put forward by the recently founded Governess Benevolent Institution. In fact, she thought it cruel to attempt to raise the standard of a governess's acquirements.

'Already governesses are not half nor a quarter paid for what they teach, nor in most instances is half or a quarter of their attainments required by their pupils. The young teacher's chief anxiety, when she sets out in life, always is to know a great deal; her chief fear that she should not know enough. Brief experience will, in most instances, show her that this anxiety has been misdirected. She will rarely be found too ignorant for her pupils.'

Finally, because she was a Brontë, handicapped by poor health and low vitality, Charlotte begs the Misses Williams not to waste their time in trying to attain manifold accomplishments for a salary of twenty pounds per annum, but to lay in a good stock of 'health, strength and cheerfulness'. She draws her portrait of the ideal governess as a strong young woman with a friendly manner and great powers of self-control. 'Fortitude and sound principles are the best aids through a governess's life,' declared Charlotte.

A month later, Mr Williams writes again to Charlotte. Although one of his daughters, Fanny, has become privately engaged to an artist, he would still like her to be a governess even though the experience might be painful for her. Charlotte calms his fears and repeats her practical counsels. By all means let Fanny go.

'If she intends to be an artist's wife she had better try an apprenticeship with Fortune as a governess first; she cannot undergo a better preparation for that honourable (honourable if rightly considered) but certainly not luxurious destiny. The experiment might do good and could not do harm, because even if she failed at the first trial (which is not unlikely) she would still be in some measure benefited by the effort.' (Haworth, 15th June 1848)

A year later, Charlotte asks Mr Williams to let his third daughter, Louisa, go to Queen's College in preparation for her governess-career. She has the perfect temperament being an obliging, cheerful and tactful young woman. She is pretty, too, 'that is always an advantage – children like it,' writes Charlotte. In fact, she thinks it would be a mistake to keep Louisa at home. Teachers might still be hard-worked, ill-paid and despised, 'but the girl who stays at home doing nothing is worse off than the hardest-wrought, and worst-paid drudge of a school'. (3rd July 1849)

With these words, Charlotte Brontë concluded her advice to Mr Williams, advice which had been the outcome of the career that had so enriched her genius.

Emily Brontë

The brief interlude that Emily Brontë spent as a governess at Miss Patchett's Academy for Young Ladies at Law Hill, near Halifax, was of great importance to her as a creative writer.

'It was partly her life in Yorkshire – the local colour was mainly derived from her brief experience as a governess at Halifax – but it was partly also the German fiction which she devoured during the Brussels period (*ie* when pupil-teacher at the Pensionnat Heger) that inspired *Wuthering Heights*,' wrote that great Brontë authority, Clement K. Shorter. In a later book on Emily Brontë, Mr Charles Simpson suppotrs Shorter's opinion with some interesting material of a topographical nature concerning Emily's stay near Halifax.

It is generally supposed that Emily left Haworth Parsonage in the early autumn of 1836 but the actual day of her departure is not known or for how long she was away. The wild and lonely place where she was a governess could only have been chosen by Emily. Not for her a rich tradesman's home, standing in sheltered grounds like Upperwood Park, nor a gentleman's comfortable manor-house like Thorp Green where Anne spent five years.

'Tis evening now, the sun descends
In golden glory down the sky;
The city's murmur softly blends
With zephyr's breathing gently by.'

E. 20* (14th October 1837)

On such an evening, Emily's gig might have drawn up before the tall, grim façade of Law Hill, Southowram, originally built in 1771 by Jack Sharp, an unscrupulous ne'er-do-well, prototype to Heathcliffe. Its high narrow windows overlooked a patch of grass, bare of shrubs or flowers. The whole house had the air of a prison; it seemed haunted. In the distance, rose the grim brow of Beacon Hill surrounded by moors, far more savage and desolate in their appearance than those that lay round Haworth. But this ominous landscape could not frighten Emily. On the contrary, it drew her; she felt at home.

'I paused on the threshold, I turned to the sky
I looked on the heaven and the dark mountain round;
The full moon sailed bright through that Ocean on high
And the wind murmured past with a wild eerie sound;
And I entered the walls of my dark prison house;
Mysterious it rose from the billowy moor.
O come with me, thus rang the song,
The moon is bright in Autumn's sky,
And thou has toiled and laboured long
With aching head and weary eye.'

D. 11 (October 1838)

We hear nothing from Emily of her exhausting life at Law Hill. For Miss Patchett extracted the last ounce of work from her teaching staff and Emily was its youngest member. Only Charlotte was anxious, writing to Ellen Nussey from Dewsbury Moor: '. . . my sister Emily is gone into a situation as teacher in a large school of near forty pupils, near Halifax. I have had one letter from her since her departure – it gives an

* These lines are dated and numbered by C. W. Hatfield whose arrangement in chronological order of Emily Brontë's *Poems* I have followed. (Publishers: The Columbia Press)

appalling account of her duties. Hard labour from six in the morning until near eleven at night, with only one half-hour of exercise between .This is slavery. I fear she will never stand it.' (2nd October 1836)

But Emily did stand it; that is the interesting point. Moreover, she emerged much stronger in health and imaginatively far the richer for her gruelling experience.

Did Emily go into the alien wilderness of a girls' school to undergo certain self-imposed tests of mental and physical endurance? She could have been a private governess in far more comfortable surroundings. I feel, myself, that the physical defeat she suffered at Roe Head rankled with Emily and any thought of experiencing family life was stifling. Emily, the stern individualist, might tolerate an order given to her by a superior teacher but what would her reaction have been to one from a silly mother?

It has been recorded that she was not unpopular with her pupils. With her tall slender figure, her cropped head and strange 'kindling' eyes, it is pretty certain Emily would have attracted most girls at their most impressionable age. Her complete indifference to what people thought of her was a considerable asset, too, in her profession.

One day, the story goes, as she stood by her blackboard, facing a class of restless pupils, she cried angrily that 'the old house-dog was dearer to her than any one of them'. In a flash, the picture of Emily Brontë as the typical, meek governess of the period is obliterated forever. She would have demanded instant obedience from her pupils as she did from her dog, 'Keeper'. Emily was that kind of person.

There was one subject, too, she would have taught superbly – natural history. Didn't she love to watch 'the blue ice curdling on the stream'? Within touch of her hands, she knew exactly where a pair of young ousels might nest. Many of the poetic similes used in *Wuthering Heights* have their root in natural history lore. For instance 'she breathed fast as a cat', or Linton Heathcliffe, 'such a cobweb, a pinch would annihilate him'. Catherine Earnshaw knew that the first spring flower at her home was the golden crocus which came with soft thaw winds and the first sunbeams. Tossing distraught on her torn pillow at Thrushcross Grange, her feverish fingers went plucking one feather after another as she murmured:

'That's a turkey's and this is a wild duck's; and this is a pigeon's. Ah! they put pigeon's feathers in the pillows – no wonder I couldn't die! Let me take care to throw it on the floor when I lie down. And here is a moorcock's; and this – I should know it among a thousand – it's a lapwing's. Bonny bird; wheeling over our heads in the middle of the moor. It wanted to get to its nest, for the clouds had touched the swells and it felt rain coming. This feather was picked from the heath, the bird was not shot . . .'

At Law Hill, Emily wrote her own 'governess' poem, akin to Charlotte's in mood and theme. Dated 4th December 1838, it is written supposedly in a classroom. Emily asks her 'harassed heart' where it will go during a short pause from work. There comes back the exquisite reply with a strange music of words and simplicity of vision, unknown to Charlotte's verses. Emily's heart flies home to :

> ' A little and a lone green lane
> That opened on a common wide ;
> A distant, dreamy, dim blue chain
> Of mountains circling every side ;
> A heaven so clear, an earth so calm
> So sweet, so soft, so hushed an air ;
> And, deepening still the dream-like charm,
> Wild moor-sheep feeding everywhere . . .'

Still, the harsh rigours of Law Hill under Miss Patchett's stern régime suited Emily in a way, while all the comfort of school life with Miss Wooler at Roe Head had left her feeling enervated and restless. When she left of her own free will in the spring of 1839, her head was stuffed full of Yorkshire tales and local legends; of a queer decaying gentry, alike but yet different to the gentry living in their own hidden valley homes round Haworth. Her flashing eyes had gazed, absorbed and fascinated, on many a crumbling stone manor-house, roofless and desolate. Particularly upon one house, High Sunderland Hall, the ancient home of the Sunderland family, which lay barely two miles away from Southowram. Its curiously carved façade and grotesque gateway, once seen as it must have been by Emily, made a vivid impression on her. There is something about this decayed shell of a house that most resembles Wuthering Heights, the home of the eccentric Earnshaws, both in its peculiar atmosphere and architecture. It obviously inspired, too, that magnificent fragment of Emily's which begins:

' Old Hall of Elbe, ruined, lonely now ;
House to which the voice of life shall ne're more return ;
Chambers roofless, desolate, where weeds and ivy grow ;
Windows through whose broken arches the night-winds sadly
    mourn ;
Home of the departed, the long departed . . . '

74, D. 10 (June 1838)

Though her governess life at Law Hill provided her with little else but hard work, her imagination grew surprisingly in power while she was away teaching. On her return home she wrote these lovely lines:

' Oh I've gone back to the days of my youth,
    I am a child once more ;
And 'neath my father's sheltering roof,
    And near the old hall door,

I watch the cloudy evening fall,
    After a day of rain ;
Blue mists, sweet mists of summer pall
    The horizon's mountain chain.

The damp stands in the long, green grass
    As thick as morning's tears ;
And dreamy scents of fragrance pass,
    That breath of other years.'

(27th July 1839)

That 'little and lone green lane' which led away to the moors was hers once more and the schoolroom door closed against that alien world of wooden desks and giggling, inattentive girls.

So one Miss Brontë escaped from Charlotte's 'gin-horse' round of governess drudgery, and when that same Miss Brontë took up her pen to write, not for the smug reading public of her day, but for all time, she completely ignored her teaching life and drew on no experience, real or imagined, gained from being a governess as Charlotte did and Anne.

Emily set *Wuthering Heights* in the reign of George III. As the daughter, then, of a country squire, Catherine Earnshaw was not sent to boarding-school but was educated at home by the village curate, Mr Shielders. Not that he could teach much to the wild Miss Earnshaw. Cathy had no lady-like accomplishments. Of what use would they have been in her short, tempestuous life? She did not play the piano or paint peculiar pictures like Jane Eyre. She did not sew exquisitely like Agnes Grey. Cathy was an outdoor girl; a fearless rider and an ardent walker. Her one pleasure lay in books. In the splendid drawing-room at Thrushcross Grange with its fine crimson carpet and crystal chandelier, she reads or is read to by her devoted husband, Edgar Linton. Her restless hands never toy with embroidery. One fierce outburst, her temper lost, and a delicate piece of needlework would have been torn violently.

Her daughter, the second Catherine, born in March 1784, supposedly, was educated by her loving and erudite father. As his child, as well as Cathy's, she was a sophisticated little thing with prettier airs and graces than her wild mother; or, so said Nelly Dean. But again, there is no mention of the younger Catherine playing the harp or pianoforte; of doing water-colour sketches or learning, like Maria Holroyd, the filagree work. No governess, poor, plain, and disconnected like Jane Eyre or meek and gentle like Miss Grey strays into the stormy world of Wuthering Heights. If she had, what would Emily Brontë have done with her, I wonder? At Thrushcross Grange, it is conceivable that a governess might have been engaged once to act as companion to Isabella Linton. But once Nelly Dean appears on the domestic scene, where would that genteel creature have been? Anyhow, Edgar Linton never tried the experiment. He knew his two Cathys. They could take a sharp scolding, even corporal punishment, from the gnarled hand and tart tongue of an old nanny, but never from a governess, that refined product of a world so alien to theirs. In the education of her two heroines, Emily Brontë is superbly right as always.

Apart from the few poems she wrote during her stay at Law Hill, poems concerned for the most part with those mystic regions of 'flowerless moors and roaring winds' where her chainless spirit roamed secure, not a shred of evidence is left to us of what she felt or thought about the profession of governess. We only know that her marvellous courage, that capacity of hers 'always to endure', scored a complete victory over those months of incessant toil at Law Hill. She returned home, assured in her mind now, that what Charlotte and Anne could do, so could she.

Anne Brontë

With her violet-blue eyes, her auburn ringlets and that consumptive flush on her delicate cheeks, Anne Brontë was by far the prettiest of the Brontë sisters. She was the most tolerant one, too, and tough in spite of her fragile air. For she made a success of governessing and endured the hardships of this most gruelling of nineteenth century professions for girls longer than either Charlotte or Emily. When we wish to know what a young governess thought, felt, or experienced in the Early Victorian schoolroom, we read *Agnes Grey* in preference to Charlotte's world-famous and glamorous *Jane Eyre*.

Anne was educated at home before going for a final polish to

Roe Head after Emily had pined there and been obliged to return home. In her nineteenth year, though, Anne's tender conscience began pricking her. She felt that she must help 'dear Papa', so sadly burdened by Branwell's debts and extravagant wish for an artist's life. So, one cold and windy day in March 1839, Anne put on her bonnet and shawl and set out in the Haworth gig across the moors to Blake Hall, where she had engaged herself to a Mrs Ingham.

Never had such a high-minded and gentle governess left her parsonage home as the youngest Miss Brontë. Anne's idealistic conception of her profession is made clear in her book when Agnes Grey, her heroine, thinks:

' How delightful it would be to be a governess ! To go out into the world ; to enter a new life ; to act for myself ; to exercise my unused faculties ; to earn my own maintenance . . .

> Delightful task !
> To teach the young idea how to shoot.'

Poor Anne! She was quickly disillusioned when she found how indifferent the spoilt little Inghams were to her lessons and beyond the control, even, of their fond mother, who appeared rather startled by the new governess's soft, stammering voice. There was nothing that Anne could do at Blake Hall but 'stick always to her first word and get along as best she could'.

When she returned at Christmas to Haworth for a well-earned holiday, she did not go back to Mrs Ingham. She told Charlotte and Emily that the children had been too much for her and that it had been 'a struggle of life-wearing exertion to keep them in anything like decent order'.

But out she went again, undeterred, in the New Year, and this time she was luckier. Her employers, the Reverend Edmund Robinson and Mrs Robinson, of Thorp Green in the Parish of Little Ouseburn in Yorkshire, were kind people. They never asked her to walk 'a little behind them' when they went to church as Charlotte had been asked to by the Sidgwicks at Stonegappe. Not that Anne's feelings would have been hurt like Charlotte's by a request of this kind. Anne Brontë became a successful governess by virtue of what Charlotte described as her 'long-suffering, self-denying, reflective and intelligent character'. Her sweet face and gentle manners completely won her pupils' hearts and the two Robinson girls corresponded affectionately with her till she died.

Thorp Green was a pleasant stone house, standing in water-meadow country where the little river Ure joined the Ouse. In the distance, rose picturesque old churches flanked by groups of slender poplars and leafy elms. The wide-open sky was of that thin, transparent blueness which is so characteristic of a flat landscape intersected by winding streams and stretches of placid water. There were clouds always, for Anne to watch at Thorp Green; enormous white-wool shapes that remained motionless for hours on end or scudded in light, small packs across the sky. Her sensitive imagination reacted to this unfamiliar world of changing light and shade, of sliding water and leafy trees, of river-banks fringed by sighing reeds instead of savage moorland stretching as far as the eye could see. Her years spent at Little Ouseburn have infused her writing with a different spirit from her sisters. Her prose style mirrors her mind; it is clear as water. Although Anne Brontë is criticised as being mistress of the commonplace, she writes with that same love of homely detail found in the miniaturist's art, and her delicate descriptions of the English countryside have all the charm of an early nineteenth century aquatint.

In the same quiet way, that she sat down and wrote, so vividly and honestly, of schoolroom life at the beginning of Queen Victoria's reign, Anne Brontë produced the most representative poems of the homesick governess, coming from a parsonage background. The theme of separation, of personal loneliness and pious devotion, inspires them all. How different are these simple but poignant verses, written while she was at Thorp Green, from Emily's lyric reply at Law Hill to 'her harassed heart' or even Charlotte's more staid *The Teacher's Monologue*.

' For yonder garden, fair and wide
With groves of evergreen,
Long winding walks, and borders trim
And velvet lawns between ;

Restore to me the little spot
With grey walls compassed round.
Where knotted grass neglected lies
And weeds usurp the ground.

Though all around this mansion high
Invites the foot to roam,
And though its walls are fair within
Oh, give me back my home ! '

With that last imploring cry, the gentle, long-suffering personality of the early Victorian governess is completely identified. Years later, Charlotte said Anne's verses had 'a sweet sincere pathos of their own', and analysed her delicate charm of writing and dove-like personality in one exquisite phrase: 'When I look round, she is in the blue tints, the pale mists, the waves and shadows of the Horizon.'

The years passed uneventfully for Anne at Thorp Green. In the spring months, she would take her girls out primrose-picking in the pretty sheltered lanes; in the winter, they kept indoors, reading instructive books or embroidering. Anne Brontë was a beautiful needlewoman.

In 1842, Branwell joined his sister at Thorp Green as tutor to the Robinsons' son. For a time, all went well; then it became apparent in the family circle at Haworth that Branwell was causing trouble at Thorp Green. His first interest in Mrs Robinson had grown into a wild obsession, induced by his unbalanced character and drug-taking habits. Unable to bear what was taking place round her, Anne left the Robinson family of her own accord, although begged to remain.

Once back at home, she joined Charlotte writing in their little front parlour while Emily scribbled, upstairs, in her monastic cell. For Anne had her own share of the Brontë genius which flowered so modestly in her novel *Agnes Grey*, that first appeared with *Wuthering Heights* in the autumn of 1847, and which George Moore declared to be 'the most perfect prose narrative in English literature'.

Agnes Grey, youngest daughter of a clergyman, goes bravely out into the world as a children's governess after her father has lost his fortune in a sea venture. She was not beautiful. Her hair was an ordinary brown colour, her complexion pale, and her eyes dark-grey. But she was an accomplished girl, according to her mother, Mrs Grey, who had helped to educate her. She could teach music, singing, drawing, French, Latin and German, for which she was paid £25 a year by Mrs Bloomfield, the wife of a retired tradesman.

Agnes was intensely unhappy with the coarse, rich Bloomfields and her sufferings are vividly described by Anne, whose simple, straightforward style, frank language, and keen, all-observing eye gives her plain tale of a period governess a terrific air of verisimilitude. She paints a grim picture of Agnes Grey wedging herself in a chair before her odious pupil whom she had to call 'Master Tom', and declining to move until he had completed his lesson; another, of his horrible little sister, Mary Ann, being forcibly held by her with one hand while her other supported the lesson-book that she refused to look at. There were, no doubt, hundreds of real governesses who resorted to these same primitive methods of exacting obedience from their rude, refractory pupils in contemporary schoolrooms. But Anne Brontë was the first writer to make fictional use of them.

Agnes Grey's second post, with a so-called aristocratic family, the Murrays of Horton Lodge, was not much better. For Mrs Bloomfield's downright rudeness, there was Mrs Murray with her politely veiled, but still poisonous little barbs of sarcasm directed always at the governess. In her opinion, all governesses 'wanted that meek spirit which St Matthew, or some of them say, is better than the putting on of apparel – you will know the passage to which I allude, for you are a clergyman's daughter'.

While employed by the selfish and wordly-minded Murrays, Agnes Grey met Edward Weston, a humble curate whom she eventually married. A quiet English gentleman lacking the dark, mysterious looks and wealth of Mr Rochester, Edward Weston symbolises the perfect marriage-partner for our heroine, the governess, because he could supply that 'quiet little vicarage with the ivy-clad porch and an old-fashioned garden', which had always been her dream-home.

In Anne Brontë's second novel, *The Tenant of Wildfell Hall*, Miss Myers portrays the flashy type of minx-governess destined to appear in many guises in nineteenth century fiction. Unlike Jane Eyre or Agnes Grey, she had a fine voice, but her mind and person was mediocre. Another Becky Sharp, she charmed Mr Huntingdon to such good purpose that he fled from Wildfell Hall with her.

Agnes Grey is not a work of genius but it has undeniable quality and could not have been written except by a governess of the period.

The slow, uncomfortable journeys forced on poor Miss Grey to reach her new posts, followed by her lonely arrivals, are extremely well done. So are those pretty descriptions of Yorkshire lanes in which she walked with her pupils and picked, one day, three lovely primroses with Edward Weston; walks that culminate in Anne Brontë's luminous word-painting of Scarborough sands, seen in the pellucid light of an early summer's morning. It was on those sands, known so well to her and above which she lies buried, that she reunites Edward Weston and Agnes.

It is Anne Brontë with her ironic sense of humour and her completely honest, unsentimental approach to life who first sets, realistically, the ordinary scene of middle-class, Victorian family life and introduces in gentle, refined Miss Agnes Grey with her 'pale hollow cheek and ordinary brown hair', the governess that was to be so cruelly exploited through the century – the clergyman's daughter.

The Misses Brontë's Establishment

FOR

THE BOARD AND EDUCATION

OF A LIMITED NUMBER OF

YOUNG LADIES,

THE PARSONAGE, HAWORTH,

NEAR BRADFORD.

Terms.

	£.	s.	d.
BOARD AND EDUCATION, including Writing, Arithmetic, History, Grammar, Geography, and Needle Work, per Annum, ...	35	0	0
French, .. German,.. Latin .. each per Quarter, ...	1	1	0
Music, .. Drawing,.. each per Quarter, ...	1	1	0
Use of Piano Forte, per Quarter, ...	0	5	0
Washing, per Quarter, ...	0	15	0

Each Young Lady to be provided with One Pair of Sheets, Pillow Cases, Four Towels, a Dessert and Tea-spoon.

A Quarter's Notice, or a Quarter's Board, is required previous to the Removal of a Pupil.

A Prospectus sent out by Charlotte Brontë on behalf of her sisters, to which no reply or bare acknowledgment was ever received.

III

CHAPTER SIX

The Victorian Governess

' The Governess is a class rapidly on the increase ; it is the only recourse left to young girls in the highest ranks of society who are forced to earn their living. She may be known from her plain and quiet style of dress ; a deep straw bonnet with green or brown veil and on her face a fixed sad look of despair.'

From a Ladies' Journal, 1840

By the time that young Queen Victoria was firmly seated on the throne, prosperous English parents had found their ideal governess, who embodied all the schoolroom virtues, in the refined and delicate girls that came from the parsonage. As their fathers were often 'younger sons' appointed to the family living and their mothers, the descendants of those seventeenth century 'gentlewomen', who first brought culture to village life and instructed the poor of their husband's parish, these girls were essentially well-bred. Connected by blood, then, to the landed gentry, the clergyman's daughter had immense snob-value to rich, middle-class parents who wished to give their rude, healthy children the polished manners of polite society through early contact with a gentlewoman. Another excellent mark in her favour was that having been early apprenticed by her mother to teaching her numerous young brothers and sisters, or the illiterate poor in her father's Sunday and Night School, she was admirably equipped to enter more profitable schoolrooms by the time she was eighteen.

Lastly, by virtue of her home background, the clergyman's daughter possessed almost the best qualification of all for her profession – a humble and meek spirit. When cruelly baited by her childish tormentors in the schoolroom, she could be trusted to remain silent and forgiving. She also knew, poor girl, the sad facts of life, the sins and violences of her father's parish having been early revealed to her.

Another type of girl governess almost as much prized as the clergyman's daughter and sacrificed in ever-increasing numbers on the Victorian governess-altar, came pale and silent as a ghost, from a suddenly impoverished home. She had little but her blue blood and aristocratic name to offer her employer. But how eagerly was she snapped up and shown off! Charlotte Brontë referred to this most unfortunate of period governesses in *Shirley* when Miss Hardman declared how: 'We need the imprudences, extravagances, mistakes, and crimes of a certain number of fathers, to sow the seed from which WE reap the harvest of governesses. The daughters of tradespeople, however well-educated, must necessarily be underbred, and as such unfit to be the inmates of OUR dwellings, or guardians of OUR children's minds and persons. We shall never prefer to place those about OUR offspring who have not been born and bred with somewhat of the same refinement as OURSELVES.'

Whether a governess belonged by birth to the Church, the Nobility, or to the Army (an officer's daughter was a welcome recruit always) her profession had never before been so exploited as in Victorian times. No governess was asked to be 'always lovely and always inviting, knowing the best books' as the Reverend John Bennett had decreed in the eighteenth century. Considering the dangerous presence of the susceptible male in the Victorian home, the children's governess must be as plain as possible. Husbands did not want clever wives or fathers brilliant daughters. They preferred them sweetly ignorant, clinging, and good. So the clergyman's daughter with her virtuous background and genteel accomplishments was admirably suited to reign in the schoolroom.

By 1845, a governess had never been so easy to distinguish with her pale, depressed look; even the clothes she wore had become a uniform. There was her all-eclipsing cottage bonnet

and her drab, all-enveloping merino shawl; her threadbare
gloves; her neatly furled umbrella and carpet-bag used when
going from one situation to another. Sad symbols, all, of her
profession.

In the Royal Academy of 1845, a picture was hung which
showed the period governess seated in her schoolroom, far
away from home. Sentimentally but exquisitely, Richard Redgrave, RA, has portrayed in 'The Poor Teacher' the delicate
girl with the long silky ringlets and black dress, who suffered
such harsh treatment at the hands of her insensitive employers.
In his brilliant *Portrait of an Age*, Mr G. M. Young has
pointed out that the figure of the governess, snubbed, bullied,
loving, and usually quite incompetent, is a stand-by of Victorian pathos. Redgrave paints that figure, of whom the
great Mr Thackeray wrote as art critic for *Fraser's Maga-
zine*: 'The Teacher's young pupils are at play in the garden,
she sits sadly in the schoolroom; there she sits, poor dear! –
the piano is open beside her, and (oh, harrowing thought!)
"Home, Sweet Home" is open in the music book. She sits and
thinks of that dear place, with a sheet of black-edged note-
paper in her hand. They have brought her tea and bread-and-
butter on a tray. She has drunk the tea, and she has not
tasted the bread-and-butter.'

Mr Thackeray knew all about governesses. Had not he
declared that 'the daughter of a clergyman' was as compact a
social statement in nineteenth century England as *'veuve de la
Grande Armée'* in nineteenth century France? Poor man! He
had suffered considerably from the steady stream of incompetent governesses passing through his home, disrupting his
life and literary work either by demands for a rise in salary or
by absorbing the attention (in the care of Miss Truelock) of
the great Miss Brontë when she came to dine in Young
Street. And what had these inadequate gentlewomen taught
his two motherless daughters? 'Three hours of Miss Colmache
isn't enough,' he had cried once in despair. On the top of all
this, he had been deeply wounded by the rumour that *Jane*

Eyre had been written by one of his daughters' governesses in mixed feelings of admiration and revenge for his having modelled – or so she thought mistakenly – the character of Becky Sharp on her. His relations, particularly his mother, had gone so far as to believe that he had cast unlawful eyes on the governess. Years later, Thackeray burst out in a letter to Mrs Sartoris, 'Whenever I hear of poor gentlemen and poor governesses accused of this easy charge, I become wild and speak no more, no doubt from a sense more of my own wrongs than theirs.' (1856)

Many Victorian parents, particularly the New Victorian Rich, cared little what their children were taught, so long as they did not speak with a provincial accent and made a pretty effect in their best bibs and tuckers when summoned to appear downstairs in the drawing room with their governess. Usually, a well-bred governess professed to teach English in all its branches, French, German and Italian; singing, music, thoroughbass; painting in oils and water-colours; pencil and chalk drawing in every style; ornamental needlework, dancing and drilling. But, how thoroughly?

During the 1840s, over one hundred governesses advertised daily in *The Times* for a situation. The highest salary demanded was £100 a year; an average one varied from £30 to £40. Some ill-equipped girls confined their teaching pretensions to 'little children only'; others took it upon themselves 'to finish without masters'. The majority offered 'the usual branches of a solid English education', while there were a few desperate advertisers who 'would impart all their gifts in exchange for a comfortable home'.

Mrs Jane Loudon, editor of *The Lady's Companion* and the authoress of many charming Victorian gardening books, gave excellent advice on *How Girls should be Educated*. 'As I have had considerable experience with both girls and governesses,' she wrote, 'may I give my reasons for thinking that under a governess is the safest, the healthiest, the pleasantest, the most effectual, and cheapest form of education?'

Cheap, yes, but too cheap – that was the tragedy. The supply of governesses far exceeded the demand now. They had become a drug on the market. By 1850, 21,000 refined gentlewomen were registered as belonging to the most despised profession in Victorian England. In spite of this staggering figure, only two miserable pensions of £15 per annum were collected for presentation in 1860, by the Governess Benevolent Institution. There were sixty-five applicants. When Florence Nightingale undertook the reorganisation of the Institution for the Care of Sick Gentlewomen in Distressed Circumstances at Number 1, Harley Street, in 1853, she told her father that governesses formed the biggest proportion of her patients because the Home was 'the cheapest lodging they can find'. Later, in 1857, her correspondence with Doctor Pincoffs reveals how her governess-patients suffered chiefly from cancer or hysteria, but: 'I had more than one lunatic. I think the deep feeling I have of the miserable position of educated women in England was gained while there.'

By her tender understanding of the Victorian governess's lonely, abnormal life, Florence Nightingale did much to alleviate the lot of those unfortunate creatures, who passed through her able hands. She always insisted on them spending a good holiday among kind people before taking up a new post. This kind of preferential treatment was unheard of then. Till the end of her long life, governesses were always writing to Miss Nightingale, feeling she was their friend and champion. Today, a psychologist would approve strongly of Florence Nightingale's efforts to rehabilitate her poor, downtrodden patients, but in the nineteenth century no one, least of all her employers, was concerned with the private life of the governess. A mere automaton in the home, she obeyed orders as they were given, without comment.

Never had a well-bred girl's chances of marriage been so poor either, once she had become a governess. Frequently, she was told that, 'Your own good sense will show you that honourable attachment is rarely formed for a Governess by a Gentleman.' Servants were habitually rude to her and, unlike the meanest skivvy in a household, she was not permitted to have 'followers'. In *The Eustace Diamonds* (1870), fond though Lady Fawn was of her sweet governess, Lucy Morris, who was a perfect lady, she warned her that if she had an admirer he must never step inside Fawn Court.

Professionally, the life of the Victorian governess was hemmed in by all sorts of petty snobberies and shibboleths that led to the complete denial of all her natural instincts. She might love her pupils and wish to express that love but the convention of her day forbade her to display any feeling towards them; neither could her pupils reciprocate her affection. Often the poor governess faced the possibility of not being able to keep her miserable pittance for herself. She could be as easily victimised by her male relations and looked on as a useful source, to supply money for buying cigars or for helping to cancel gambling debts in the same way that slum children were forced into 'sweated labour' to support their gin-sodden parents. This is illustrated in the case of Miss White, governess in the Stanley family.

Her story begins with the strong-minded Lady Stanley of Alderley Park in Cheshire writing to her Irish daughter-in-law, Henrietta, married to her son, Edward, 'It does seem wonderful that good or even tolerable governesses should be so scarce and that their expectations should be so exorbitant in times when one might suppose many would wish for a governess who cannot afford to pay them high, and that very many well-educated persons must be wanting bread. I am much afraid that you will not get *all* you require under £100 – but certainly my own opinion is that so very few governesses are capable of *teaching everything* that I should prefer a humbler *professor* at 80 and spend the remaining 20 in Masters. They are sufficiently grounded in German to be able to go on with the language – Musick is the only thing a governess ought to know enough of to keep them well up in their practising, but I must say I do not think they have musical bumps.

'It certainly seems to me they want most general knowledge and a sensible woman about them who will improve their minds and be able to converse with them on what they read or see and above all one who will take an interest in them and not like Mdlle R throw them off entirely except at lessons.

'I quite agree with you that the *manners* of a gentlewoman are *essential*, especially as they generally though not always prove the *mind* of one besides.

'Poor Koelle was found dead in the ice-house gardens, there is something mysterious about her end – Louise fancies she had been drinking *bullocks blood*.' (28th March 1843)

The next thing we hear after Koelle's intriguing demise is the engagement of a Miss Eccles as governess to the Stanley girls. She is lazy, loathes walking, and young Mrs Stanley tells Lady Stanley 'has only been outside the door three times in this week of lovely weather'.

So Miss Eccles departs. Four months later old Lady Stanley asks her daughter-in-law: 'How is it that you cannot hear of any governess at all – have you seen any? I am afraid it will be a difficulty as indeed you find it having such a large family. I expect, at last, rather than have no help you will be obliged to take a moderately accomplished person and trust to Masters when you can get them or to the girls hereafter improving themselves when older.'

At last, though, a suitable governess called Miss White was found who sounded 'Almost too perfect to be true – most satisfactory certainly – not playing herself an advantage I think as she will not want to practise. I do hope you are well suited.' (10th March 1844)

Young Mrs Edward was more than well suited. But her naïve, Irish enthusiasm met with the usual salutary douche of cold water from her cynical mother-in-law.

'Very glad you are pleased with Miss White. Hope it will

continue – but I think you praised Miss Eccles' sense at first however I daresay this is quite a different person.' (25th March 1844)

Later in the same satirical vein, came this: 'I am very glad you continue to like Miss White so much, now you have seen more of her – I do hope the girls will gain and keep hold of some information and learn to speak and write English.'

The little Miss Stanleys were kept well hidden in the school-room, on the few occasions that their father was at home. There was always one question uppermost in Henrietta Stanley's mind, and that was how to prise money out of her absent Edward to meet her housekeeping bills. Things came to a pretty pass one day when Miss White's salary was in jeopardy.

Winnington Aug. 9th, 1846

'My dearest Love,

I was sure you would be grieved to hear of Johnny's delicate state of health – I observed last night when saying his prayers how short his breath was . . .

Do you think you could give Miss White £20, we owe her a quarter. She did not ask for it but I saw she was in distress and Alice told me that her brother wanted £20 and could not get it from people that owed it to him. If you send it to her she would I am sure be thankful.'

Ten days later Miss White's salary was still unpaid. Was there a Victorian governess alive who dared protest at such casual treatment? The whole incident shows how the poor creatures were not only considered fair game by their relatives for borrowing from, but how casually their own employers treated them in the matter of payment. No wonder Mrs Jameson, the well known writer on social and educational questions of this time, declared how she had 'never heard of a governess who was such by choice.'

Mrs Jameson took up the governess-cause warmly and

gave some excellent advice in the chapter on the 'Relative Position of Mothers and Governesses' that was incorporated in her *Memoirs and Essays*, published in 1860. She tells the governess, among many other things, how to dress. 'Perfect neatness, a simplicity not without elegance will be found more ladylike and economical. A young governess is apt to over-dress in the part. An older one to skimp. But whatever salary yours is, put by the half of it if you can; a third – a quarter – something be it ever so little.'

Jane Eyre's plain stuff dress and merino pelisse with a grey silk for festive occasions was in perfect governess taste. The day after Mr Rochester's proposal we know that she put on her lilac gingham to express her happiness but when he tried to buy her a length of superb pink satin and a rich amethyst silk, she insisted on having a sober black satin and a pearl-grey silk instead.

One Victorian governess was told by her exacting employer 'to wear constantly a high dress with a frill. She thought she might venture to remark, the black ribbon round her neck rather savoured of coquetry. It seemed so palpably designed to contrast with the hue of her skin.'

Like Charlotte Brontë, Mrs Jameson was all against a higher education for governesses. 'What is the point to fit a woman for a private governess? You must not only cram her with grammar, languages, and dates and all the technicalities of teaching but educate her in the seclusion of a nunnery and inure her to privation, discipline and drudgery; and above all the cruelty – yes, that is the word – the cruelty of giving her ideas, nay, feelings, aspirations which might render the slavery of her future more dreadful than of necessity it must be.'

Mrs Jameson drew notice for the first time to that persistently ignored room – the schoolroom. It had never occurred even to conscientious Victorian parents that a well-equipped, pleasant room should be set aside for the governess and her pupils.

'A schoolroom', declared Mrs Jameson, 'should be large and airy. How often are they the opposite!' She proceeds to describe one that she had seen in a lord's town house. 'You went up a backstairs to a small set of rooms with a confined gloomy aspect; the study was barely furnished and a carpet faded and mended, stiff-backed chairs as if for penance – a large table against the wall, a map of Europe and the Stream of Time, – a look of meanness, coldness, bareness which would have chilled at once any woman accustomed to a home who had known the habits and accessories of elegant life.'

Lessons were still extremely dull and limited. Indifferent French was taught and the elegant gilt harp had given way to a rosewood pianoforte. The 'use of the globes' continued and Miss Richmal Mangnall's *Questions* constituted the governess's teaching bible along with Doctor Butler's *A Key to Knowledge*. Instead of those delightful hand-coloured copy-books used in the eighteenth century, there were drab brown paper ones in which little girls made endless rows of emasculated pot-hooks and hangers and later copied proverbs like 'pride goes before a fall' or 'train up a child in the way it should go'. For hornbooks there were now squeaking slates and the blackboard.

According to *The Governess*, published by Charles Knight in 1844, a member of the teaching profession should know 'something of music, something of French'. Unreasonable employers might press for 'a little drawing and something of general literature'. In his helpful hints on *First Lesson for the Very Young*, Mr Knight urges the good governess to stick to writing. 'Keep them to the stroke till they represent them correctly; there is no need to be in a hurry about them.'

In the Victorian schoolroom, time was of no object, for the taking of public exams or school certificates by young ladies were still undreamt of. Gradually though, Mr Knight's amateurish methods of helping governesses to clarify the mysteries of subtraction and addition with the aid of ivory counters, marbles and even apples and oranges came to be frowned on. Globes were considered inadequate and super-seded by shiny, new embossed maps. With the popularity of nigger minstrels, fashionable young ladies took to having lessons on the banjo and new accomplishments taught by the Governess were Pokerwork, Floral Painting on Velvet and Glass and Berlin Woolwork soon the rage. No one has summed up, so perfectly, the education of a Victorian girl as Elizabeth Barrett Browning in her long narrative poem, *Aurora Leigh*. From Italy, the orphaned Aurora, comes home to England, to live with a maiden aunt in the country where:

> ' I learnt the collects and the catechism,
> The creeds, from Athanasius back to Nice,
> The Articles . . . The Tracts against the times
> (By no means Buonaventure's " Prick of Love "),
> And various popular synopses of
> Inhuman doctrines never taught by John,
> Because she liked instructed piety.
> I learnt my complement of classic French
> (Kept pure of Balzac and neologism),
> And German also, since she liked a range
> Of liberal education, – tongues, not books.
> I learnt a little algebra, a little
> Of the mathematics, – brushed with extreme flounce
> The circle of sciences, because
> She misliked women who are frivolous.
> I learnt the royal genealogies
> Of Oviedo, the internal laws
> Of the Burmese empire . . . ,
> I learnt much music, – such as would have been
> As quite impossible in Johnson's day
> As still it might be wished – and I drew costumes
> From French engravings, nereids neatly draped
> With smirks of simmering godship, – I washed in
> From nature, landscapes (rather say, washed out),
> I danced the polka and Cellarius,
> Spun glass, stuffed and modelled flowers in wax,
> Because she liked accomplishments in girls . . .
> I learnt cross-stitch, because she did not like
> To see me wear the night with empty hands,

A-doing nothing. So, my shepherdess
Was something after all (the pastural saints
Be praised for't) leaning love-lorn with pink eyes
To match her shoes, when I mistook the silks : '
Aurora Leigh, 1856

An invalid, Elizabeth Barrett was educated at home and must have known a governess after the pattern of the one who taught Aurora.

When the great Mr Dickens and Mrs Fanny Kemble began giving their popular readings, elocution was taken up in a big way by primly pinafored little girls, who stood with hands folded neatly behind their backs and toes well turned out, reciting to their elders and betters gathered in the drawing-room, 'The Wreck of the Hesperus' or 'Casablanca' from *The Juvenile Reciter*.

Soon after the middle of the century, parents were recommended healthier exercise for their daughters than a mild game of shuttle-cock and battledore on the lawn. So the science of callisthenics came to be studied by the Victorian governess. She had to take charge of the dancing lessons given in the drawing-room, when she sat, stiffly upright, at the piano playing the waltz, the schottische and the polka for her pupils. And then, suddenly, like a bombshell, parents were advised that 'no professional teacher under twenty-five should be engaged for girls over fourteen who cannot produce a certificate from a University'.

Here was grim food for governess-thought! Poor Miss Benson and Miss Cholmondeley, genteel but certificateless. What on earth were they to do?

Forcefully, Miss Charlotte Yonge took up their cause. In an endless stream of novels and pamphlets, she tried to better the governess's social standing. Portraits of lovely governesses and plain governesses, governesses good, bad and indifferent, crowd the pages of her novels. Charlotte Yonge has contributed more than any other female writer to the great gallery of governesses in fiction.

In *Hopes and Fears*, the character of Miss Fennimore skilfully portrays the new type of finishing governess who
thought it an insult 'to be offered a pupil below her teens or
to lose one till nearly above them'. Charlotte Yonge wrote
about 'the pathetic governess' too, with her aggressive
counterpart, 'the wooden, unsympathetic person always imparting information of the wrong kind!' Her pet governess-
theories are best set out in *Womankind*, published in 1876.
Over and over again, she asserts that a governess is a lady
with a profession as much as a barrister is a gentleman with
a profession. Insolence to a governess is an old stock complaint.

'In real life I have never heard of it from anyone by birth
or breeding a lady. Persons with no consideration for those
about them are to be found in any rank of life; but where a
lady is forgetful of little pleasures or comforts for her governess, she is probably no better towards her husband, her
friends, or anyone she is afraid of . . .'

Charlotte Yonge never minced matters. A strong-minded
realist, her advice to all employers of that domestic bugbear
of her day, was never to sentimentalise over her situation and
to treat her as the lady she should be.

'Whether the condition of governesses ever receives the
change that is talked of depends not on employers, but on
themselves; upon their efficiency; and on their self-respect –
by which I mean by no intent that punctilio which wounds
at all points, but by that simplicity which knows its place and
is not easily provoked.'

In 1864, the first public appeal was made on the Governess's behalf by John Ruskin at the Town Hall, Manchester.
This was an event destined to make governess-history.

'Give your girls not only noble teachings, but noble
teachers. You consider somewhat before you send your boy
to school, what kind of a man the master is; whatsoever kind
of man he is, you at least give him full authority over your
son and show some respect to him yourself; if he comes to

dine with you, you do not put him at a side-table ... But what teachers do you give your girls, and what reverence do you choose to show the teachers you have chosen? Is a girl likely to think her own account or her own intellect of much importance, when you trust the entire formation of her character, moral and intellectual, to a person whom you let your servants treat with less respect than they do your house-keeper (as if the soul of your child were a less charge than jams, jellies and groceries) and on whom you yourself think you confer an honour by letting her sometimes sit in the drawing-room in the evening?'

Immediately, Victorian parents were set thinking seriously. For the daily governess hurrying to her next appointment had long been one of London's saddest sights. With her umbrella neatly furled, her long cloak, muddy at the hem, and a bundle of books carried under one arm, she was out from seven in the morning to seven or eight at night. If she happened to meet with one of her pupils, she was generally cut dead by her.

A writer in *The Young Ladies' Friend* (1840) attacked the period school-girl on this very point, saying, 'Can there be any sense in the half-educated daughter of a lawyer or merchant treating her more mature and accomplished teacher as an inferior by passing her in the street without acknow-ledging the acquaintance?'

In *The Channings* (1862), Mrs Henry Wood wrote: 'A Daily Governess! It is really only another name for a servant.' Her heroine, pretty blue-eyed Constance Channing, had to go out as one. She received £40 a year as her salary and arrived punctually at 7 am each morning to teach the two daughters of Lady Augusta Yorke.

Miss Harriet Martineau gave all the publicity she could through her books to alleviate the daily governess's unhappy lot.

'Wet or fine, they must appear as the clock strikes,' she told the world, adding that it was quite beyond the means of any daily governess to take a cab; as it was, she had to budget for spending at least £8 a year on bus fares. The best salary she could hope to achieve might be £120 a year by working non-stop, but more likely it would be only a mere £70. To assist the daily governess, trudging wearily to and from her different points of work, The Ladies' Reading Room at Langham Place was opened. Here she could rest her aching feet for an odd half-hour between her appointments, read the papers, and enjoy the amenities of a wash and brush-up.

Claire Claremont gave a vivid sketch of the trials of being a daily governess in London in a letter to Mary Shelley: 'I am so worried I fear I shall go out of my mind – this is now my life – I go by nine to Mrs Kitchener's house where I give lessons until one – then I rush to the top of Wilton Place and get a Richmond omnibus and go to Richmond to the Cohens – their daughter is going to marry a Genoese and must have an Italian lesson every day ... that vile omnibus takes two hours to get to Richmond and the same to come back and so with every giving my lesson I am never back before seven.'

Four hours wasted in transit. Four precious hours of earning capacity for Claire and every other governess. No wonder their yearly income rarely reached £80.

Twenty years later, in 1883, another brilliant young girl, Eugenie Sellers, imbued like Claire Claremont with brains and vitality, but to outdistance her far in classical scholarship, was pacing the streets of London as a daily governess. 'Pupils were abundant, terms liberal, my energy in full activity – only the work exhausting to mind and body. The London omnibus that took me from pupil to pupil, the London winter weather, both remain a nightmare.'

By the end of the century, though, after the founding of the Governess Benevolent Institution to provide for the appalling financial distress among governesses due largely to their incompetency and by the formation of evening classes given free by professors of King's College, London, the governess profession improved rapidly. Fashion now stepped in on her side and decreed a new wardrobe. Her drab bonnet and long merino cloak were relegated to the attic cupboard and the 'new look' governess appeared. In a neatly striped Garibaldi blouse, with mannish tie and flat straw-boater, she played tennis and croquet with her older pupils and dined downstairs with them *en famille*. Her schoolroom became a centre of growing importance in the home. Windows were flung open and fresh air and sunlight streamed in; a course of beauty treatment followed. Flower vases adorned the mantelpiece and new chintzes were bought to cover the dingy old horse-hair sofa that had once been considered quite good enough for the governess. No wonder she became a popular heroine in contemporary fiction! In Rosa Nouchette Carey's *Only the Governess*, published in 1888, the heroine, Miss Huldah Rossiter, is quite a ravishing beauty with her Irish dark-grey eyes like Emily Brontë's, and her thick coils of reddish brown hair. The schoolroom in which she is found teaching motherless little Dossie Weston, is just the place Mrs Jameson would have approved of.

'Schoolrooms were always ugly but this one looked like a drawing-room. There were so many pretty things about, pictures and china and handsome bookcases; there was a couch too; and delightful easy chairs and flowers on the table; a great bowl of scarlet anemones, and a china basket full of daffodils.'

But if the governess-star was shining more brightly in the sky at home, it was positively flaming abroad.

From the middle of the nineteenth century there were few Austrian castles set in romantic pine forests beside a lake, green as emerald, or a fairy-tale, French château, rising above a lilied moat, that did not boast a resident English governess round whose figure, like small moths about a candle-flame, revolved an obedient generation of little counts and countesses. The manners of the 'English Mees', as she came to be called, were above reproach and her loyalty to the noble family she served, unquestionable. As for the hand placed so firmly on her temperamental pupil's wriggling shoulder, it was gloved in the best English deerskin and had such a steadying influence. Her lessons might still be reminiscent of an old-fashioned Young Ladies' Academy in Bath or Cheltenham – but did it matter? 'Not at all,' murmured Madame la Comtesse, knowing how conscientiously *'chère Mees Smith'* would deal with the immature flirtations of her naughty little Sophy Clementine and how safe that child would always be with her.

Unsuspectedly, a gigantic fifth column operated by a devoted body of genteel ladies and apple-cheeked nannies, which was to exercise enormous power and disseminate the traditional English way of life through European society, had sprung into being.

'Is it part of the system?' asked Madame Valtesi in *The Green Carnation*, published in 1894. 'I don't know,' answered Lady Locke. 'What system do you mean?'

'The English Governess System. Simple clothes, no friends, no society, no late dinners, supper at nine, all the talents, and bed at ten whether you are inclined for it or not.'

Poor woman, she was puzzled and quite rightly! For it *was* the system, our rigidly conservative and spartan English Governess System that led inevitably to her Glorious Apotheosis abroad during which period she became a figure of almost national importance and founded a dynasty.

CHAPTER SEVEN

The English Governess Abroad

One Tuesday in March 1815, two elegant ladies stepped into a small rowing boat, bobbing up and down in the Bay of Villefranche. They were followed by a small, undistinguished female gripping her two charges, a boy and a girl, firmly by the hand.

That same evening, Lady Charlotte Bury, Lady-in-Waiting to Her Royal Highness, Princess Caroline, who was now on the Continent, wrote in her journal:

'Tuesday, March 21st, 1815
I have met Madame Davidoff and we rowed across the Bay of Villefranche. A Miss Esterly, the governess of the Davidoff children, a poor, quiet, little personage who seems estimable, but very miserable accompanied us; yet not miserable through Madame Davidoff, but because a governess is always a miserable situation and she hates the Governor. If she be a superior (and who would like to place an inferior-minded one about their children?), a governess is apt to gain such an influence over her pupils that the mother becomes jealous. The governess is treated like a servant, and as if she was not fit to live with ladies and gentlemen, though she is chosen to bring up the dearest objects of affection.'

Quite possibly, Lady Charlotte has drawn the first portrait of the English governess abroad in her journal. Little Miss Esterly soon vanishes from our sight across the Bay of Villefranche, but there follows in the wake of her boat, flock after ghostly flock of genteel ladies, though there are some vulgar exceptions, of course, who left England in the nineteenth century to gain a complete stranglehold of the most exclusive schoolrooms in the world.

It is extraordinary how far they went; many to the utmost corners of the globe. They went to earn their livelihood; that genteel livelihood, which poor gentlewomen were finding very hard to earn at home where better teaching methods than theirs were demanded. But some went for the adventure as well, emulating the spirit of their swashbuckling Elizabethan ancestors. During the nineteenth century our reputation abroad stood very high and the snob-value of acquiring a respectable and well-connected English governess was recognised by all upper-class foreign families

When that astute native ruler, King Mongkut of Siam, saw how the lion power of British Imperialism was spreading everywhere in the East, his immediate action was to introduce an English governess into his household. So Mrs Anna Leonowens found herself engaged, in 1862, to teach King Mongkut's numerous progeny in what must have been one of the queerest schoolrooms – the interior of a great temple, patrolled by a sacred, violet and crimson-bellied snake.

Not only did Anna emerge triumphant from fighting one domestic battle after another with the tyrannical king, but she ended in supervising his whole diplomatic correspondence, including his private letters to Queen Victoria. A remarkable feat for only a governess to have achieved.

At much the same time that Anna Leonowens was being a governess in Siam, Miss Emily Payne left England for even a queerer out-post than Bangkok on the global map. She went to Lashio where the long Burma-China road begins its snaky track, taking, no doubt, her green-lined sunshade, her sketch-book, and a brand-new copy of Maria Graham's (Lady Callcott) *Little Arthur's History of England* which had just been published. Miss Payne went to be a governess in the family of Hsipaw Sawbwa, the local Shan Chief, and she never returned home.

One of the most interesting features of our governess-penetration abroad is the way the English Miss, a creature of such routine and habit, church-loving and moral, rooted herself in the establishment where she was employed. Dressed first in a rustling crinoline of stiff black bombazine, later in a suit of neat serge or Harris tweed, she not only influenced one but two – sometimes even three – generations and usually ended by speaking her native tongue with the accent of her self-adopted country. One finds the German Fräulein and the French Mam'selle returning to die in their native land, but how rarely our lean Miss Bensons and Miss Cholmondeleys.

The character of the English governess abroad combines, most subtly, I think, the pioneer spirit and the missionary's zeal. She is nearly always deeply religious. If one looks for Miss Emily Payne today, she will be found in a little hill-top cemetery near Lashio. Where most of the graves lie level with the parched earth, marked only by wooden discs with numbers painted on them, Emily's grave stands out, proudly different from the rest. It bears a simple cross on which are carved these words: EMILY PAYNE Lady Governess.

But long before Emily Payne was laid to rest in remote Lashio, Lady Charlotte Bury might have come across another English governess, if she had visited Pisa after leaving Villefranche. This governess could never have been described as quiet or little; poor, yes, and miserable. But miserable only on the grand, romantic scale and burning with fiery ideals, Shelley-bred. This governess whom Lady Charlotte would have found striding moodily about Pisa's narrow streets, was Claire Clairmont, ex-mistress of Lord Byron, and the unhappy mother of Allegra, their illegitimate daughter whom she had just surrendered to him.

It was Lady Mountcashell, known as Mrs Mason to the group of English intellectuals living in Pisa, who kept urging Claire to give up teaching English and go to Vienna, as a proper, whole-time governess. Margaret Mason, a brawny middle-aged lady with a mild, beaming face and carriage 'stiff as a grenadier', loved to give advice. The eldest daughter of an Irish peer, Lord Kingsborough, her governess for a time had been Mary Wollstonecraft, mother of Mary Shelley. Through this connection she was drawn to her daughter and to Claire Clairmont.

But Claire frankly admitted that teaching other people's children bored her; as she wondered what to do next with her life, she heard of Allegra's sudden death at the Convent School near Ravello. Next came the appalling news of Shelley's drowning in the Gulf of Spezzia. Shelley who was her only genuine friend and supporter. For weeks her Journal remained empty. Then, on Friday, 20th September, came this momentous entry: 'Get up at five, pack; breakfast. It pours with rain.'

A few hours later, sunk in misery, Claire stared blindly through the streaming window of the stage coach which was bound for Vienna. Soon the country which had robbed her of the two she most loved, would be left far behind. Years after, on remembering this day, she wrote to Mary Shelley: 'Thank God, I can never be young again. At least, that suffering is spared me.'

In Vienna, her enthusiastic and always optimistic brother, Charles Clairmont, had found her suitable lodgings. He wanted to find her a situation, too; English governesses were in great demand and he had the entrée to the most exclusive Austrian circles where families like the Esterhazys and Choteks were ardently pro-English.

But Claire had other plans. Grief made her restless and she longed to leave those who knew her. Moscow called her. Imperial Moscow, that sinister city which lay buried in snow half the year. What greater contrast could she find, to sunny friendly Italy? English governesses were as much the rage in Moscow as in Vienna though 'to be a governess in Russia was the equivalent of taking the veil or a lady-like form of suicide,' wrote Mrs Gaskell in *Wives and Daughters*.

On her arrival in Moscow, then, in the summer of 1824, Claire engaged herself as a governess in the family of Zachar Nikolaevitch, a well-known lawyer with aristocratic connections. Many foreign teachers were employed by Russians to give the right cachet to home-education which was *de rigueur* in upper-class families. They were well treated and Claire's position in the Nikolaevitch household was similar to Selina Trimmer's at Chatsworth. She had two pupils; a boy called John, and a little girl, Dunia.

Life passed pleasantly. In the evenings, there were parlour games or analytical discussions took place round the samovar. Always a talker, Claire was in her element now; her dark, animated face and witty tongue attracted the Russians. But as the circles in which she moved were political, she could not admit, she confesses to her journal, how 'the charming Miss Clairmont, considered by all to be the model of good sense, accomplishment, and good taste, was brought up, issued from the very den of Free-thinkers.'

Neither could she divulge her strange secret of having been Lord Byron's mistress and the mother of his illegitimate daughter, Allegra.

Mischievously, she would sigh, sometimes, and beg to be excused from attending a party; her plea, a convenient headache. There was a fascinating air of mystery about Miss Clairmont, people declared. A mystery that Miss Clairmont was determined to preserve.

Suddenly though, tragedy came sweeping back into her life, recalling poignant memories of the past. Little Dunia fell desperately ill. Where Claire, the mother, had been banished from her dying daughter's bedside, Claire, the governess, took up her position beside her sinking pupil. All through that fatal night, she watched till dawn broke when little Dunia, 'smiling and brilliant as a star lay in a sweet stillness before us'.

After the child's death, Claire heard of Byron's tragic end in Greece and then, how Trelawny lay desperately ill in his mountain cave. Too unhappy to concentrate on her work and finding the once agreeable round of entertaining Russian Army officers entirely out of key with her mood, Claire characteristically dismissed all Russians as 'stupid, vain and ignorant' and their offspring as 'little barbarians'.

She had no intention she declared, of succumbing to the fate of the many ageing governesses, who collected like vultures 'ravenous and open-mouthed after places' in Princess Ourousoff's rooms. So she engaged herself as companion to a Madame Kaisaroff and her daughter, Natalie, and left Russia in 1828.

Later in the year she returned to London and looked up her old friends, Mary Shelley and Jane Williams, now Jane Hogg. But she was soon off again to Dresden. 'I do not, like our Mary, sail my steady course like a ship under a gentle and favourable wind,' she wrote. 'But at thirty I shall be better, and every year I hope to gain in value.'

The years came and went with her working, always working as a governess or as a paid companion. She is in Carlsbad one year; the next in Nice. In the 1840s we catch a glimpse of her, already described, as a daily governess in London. She admitted frankly to Jane Hogg that she dressed badly and acknowledged the gift of a gown from her rather grudgingly. 'It is by far too elegant for me, consequently I have put it by in the piece ... I make it a rule never to buy anything for a gown that costs more than a paul a bracchio – 12 bracchio serves me and my gown costs 12 pauls. To be sure, it is dark and coarse. I am in the land of silks but they are not for me.'

Touchy of being patronised and liable to long bouts of depression which she called her *accidie*, Claire made an uncomfortable friend. But she never moaned in the face of disaster or took offence at the way people treated her, lashing out only in a violent Claire-mood: 'I never thought that children could be so hideous or vicious, they never cease brawling, squabbling, and fighting, from morning till night.'

While visiting her old friend, Mrs Mason, in Pisa, Claire heard that cholera was raging in Vienna where she had planned to go next. She applied for the post of companion to Lady Mulgrave, wife of the newly-appointed Governor of Jamaica, writing her own reference. 'Many people would be glad of a well-informed person who can read to them in various languages, teach them German, write their letters, and of a lively, sprightly disposition, one who never minds heat or cold, nor hunger or thirst, nor fatigue, nor hardship of any kind.'

But Claire did not go to Jamaica. She remained with the Masons in Pisa and resumed her English lessons. It was the same old trudge that she had known in London. From early morning till late at night she was out teaching at one Italian house or another. But in spite of all her efforts, she managed to earn little more than £36 a year. For a time, she tried to augment this tiny income by writing and then, restless as ever, she returned to England and went as a governess to a family living at Wingfield Park where Trelawny wrote to her, 'What are you doing with the Bennets or the Sandfords? Are you always to be in this vile servitude . . . are your fetters never to be knocked off? – your pettycoats I mean . . .'

But release from governessing was on its way. Oddly enough, when her legacy of £12,000 left to her by Shelley materialised on his father's death, Claire became tetchy and querulous where in adversity she had been brave and witty.

She lived permanently in Florence, first at 83 Via Valfonda and then later in the Via Romana, looked after by her Clairmont niece, Paula. 'La fille aux mille projets,' as Shelley had once described her in those far-off, Pisan days, had become a 'small distinguished, very English lady with white curls', who told blunt truths to friends and delighted in writing disagreeable letters to Mary Shelley.

Claire Clairmont is the perfect prototype, I think, of the independent English spinster who was to be found indulging her literary tastes on a small private income in many a

Riviera pension till the Second World War of 1939 put paid utterly to this way of life.

Claire died on 19th March 1879, at the age of ninety-one. She was neither a bad governess nor a very good one. But she was never one to quarrel with her daily bread-and-butter. She was a wonderful 'mixer' too, devoid of all class snobbery and pettiness of mind. Holding her head high in adversity, Claire Clairmont managed to convey a romantic sense of mystery which never failed to intrigue foreign society where she is always found at her best.

At much the same time that Claire Clairmont was being a governess in Russia, another young Englishwoman, destined to become Brazil's first and last Imperial Governess, had sailed into the lovely Bay of Rio de Janeiro on 13th March 1823.

Like Claire, Maria Graham was slender, dark, vivacious and an ardent intellectual; like Claire, too, she had been left tragically alone in the world, having lost her adored husband, Captain Thomas Graham, RN, whilst on foreign service. Her portrait by Lawrence shows courage in the gallant set of her graceful head over whose short brown curls is worn a simple gauze turban; intelligence and humour in her alert gaze; generosity in her well-cut mouth with its short upper-lip. An entrancing head it is, of much charm and sensibility.

When Admiral Lord Cochrane in whose ship Maria had come from Chile where her husband had been buried, left Rio to raise the Siege of Bahia, Maria asked to wait upon the newly crowned Empress of Brazil in the hope that she might 'consider her as protecting her while in her Empire'. Her request was granted. With Lord and Lady Amherst en route to India, Maria was received by the gentle Empress at the Palace of San Cristovao.

'She spoke to me so kindly; and she said in a flattering way, that she had long known me by name, and several other things that persons of rank can make so agreeable by voice and manner; and I left her with the most agreeable impressions. She is extremely like several persons of the Austrian Imperial family, and has a remarkably sweet expression.'

The Empress Leopoldina, elder sister to Marie Louise, Napoleon's wife, had been married very young to Prince Pedro of Branganza, then Regent of Brazil. In his early thirties, now, with melting black eyes and a small voluptuous mouth, the Emperor was a handsome, dashing but unstable man. Full of animal fire, every court lady was out to capture his fickle heart. But just at the time of Maria Graham's arrival, the Emperor had begun his famous liaison with the brilliantly clever Dona Domitila de Castro e Mello whose husband, an officer of the Imperial Guard, had tried to kill her in a fit of jealousy. Leopoldina, a complete contrast to the raven-haired Domitila, being plump and fair and devoid of all guile, received her at court where she was treated as the Emperor's official mistress. It was best, thought the Empress, to close her gentle eyes to her husband's infidelities, particularly as she adored him. Erudite, with a large library of books on mathematics and entomology, her two pet subjects, Leopoldina had brought three drawing-masters to Rio from Vienna. Under their guidance, she was making a study of Brazilian flowers and plant life. It was only natural that the Empress, isolated with her intellectual tastes in her husband's raffish court, took an immediate liking to the talented English-woman. But soon after their meeting Maria Graham fell ill. Deeply depressed, she recorded in her journal how in Brazil, young women present nuts on St John's Eve like her Scottish countrywomen at Halloween. 'They put their hands, blind-fold on a table, with the letters of the alphabet; and practise many a simple conjuration ... For me I only wish for the nucca drop of Arab to fall this night, so I might catch it, and be relieved from my weary sickness.'

Poor Maria! Later in July, she is still plunged in gloom for 'I cannot interest myself in the little things of other people's lives as I used to do; I require the strong stimulus of public interest to rouse my attention.' Little did she dream

how soon she was going to be the centre of a perfect maelstrom of court intrigues. But she roused herself to drive out
to San Cristovao to make a sketch, promised for the Empress.
The Palace placed on rising ground in a rich, fertile valley,
was built in the Moorish style and coloured yellow with white
mouldings. Maria's drawing shows the fairy-tale character of
San Cristovao with its beautiful screen and gateway of Portland stone. During her visit she met the young Princesses,
and thought the eldest one, Dona Maria da Gloria, most
intelligent. Whilst chatting with her, the Empress appeared
and sympathised sweetly on Mrs Graham's recent illness.

Early in September, Maria moved into Rio from her cottage
out at Botafoga Bay and spent much time in the Public
Library studying Brazilian history. Then, on the 12th October, the Emperor's birthday, she rose early and went to the
Royal Chapel where their Imperial Majesties were to be with
the court before the drawing-room. Again she was singled
out by the Empress who indulged in a long conversation
with her on English authors. 'If I had been pleased with her
before,' wrote Maria Graham later in her journal, 'I was
charmed with her now.' The Empress wore a beautiful white
dress, embroidered with gold, and a cap trimmed with green-
tipped feathers. Her diamonds were magnificent and sparkled
as she moved. On withdrawing from the Royal presence,
Maria saw her most intimate Brazilian friend, Madame do
Seco Rio, speak earnestly to Her Majesty. In confidence she
had told Madame do Seco Rio that she would have liked
to educate little Dona Maria da Gloria as she was such an
intelligent child and then had thought no more about it.
But now, the Empress beckoned her back to her side and
asked her to apply to the Emperor for the post of Imperial
Governess. 'She said, "Write if you please, but come and see
the Emperor at five o'clock tomorrow." I remained mar-
velling at the chance that had brought me into a situation so
unlike anything I had ever contemplated.'

Maria Graham wrote her letter, saw the Emperor next

day, and on 16th October received a note from Leopoldina written in English. Full of kind expressions she accepted her services as governess to her daughter and gave her leave to go to England before taking up her post.

Three days later, Maria Graham was in the packet, bound for England where she was to wind up her affairs and get equipment for the imperial schoolroom. Arriving in London, she ordered a special translation to be made into Portuguese of Mrs Barbauld's *Little Charles*, and bought two huge Carey globes and some special instruments for recording the weather which she knew would appeal to the Empress.

In the midst of her shopping activities, she received a communication from her ministerial friend, Don Jose Bonifaco, to inform her that her year's leave of absence had been reduced to six months – 'for want of a European Gentlewoman in the Princess's apartments had grown serious.' Hot upon this letter, there arrived at her London lodging, two sallow-skinned Senhors representing the Brazilian Government. They urged her to return to Rio at once. Very much concerned by all this mystery, Maria decided to sail immediately.

Before she left, her friend, Miss Maria Edgeworth, the authoress of so many Cautionary Tales, sent her a characteristic letter urging her most strongly to 'Look once, look twice, look three times before you leap and before you trust yourself to a new Court in a new world. Dame d'Honneur sounds well : a *Gouvernante des Enfants de Brazil* very grand. But be clear before you take the weight or labour and responsibility that is to hang on this title, that there is a solid well-secured remuneration balancing the weight on the other side ... Whatever you agree for, put in writing, for verbal agreements, though mighty pleasant and made with a smile on the face and flattery on the lips, at Court or Drawing Room, are after all precarious tenures, and in short there is no building upon them any but castles in the air.'

But Maria had no intention of changing her plans at the

last moment and letting the Empress down. Her Brazilian castle in the air looked solid enough while Leopoldina's gentle smile lured her on to occupy it.

Within thirty-two days of Don Jose Bonifaco's communication, Maria was back in Rio, where several events had taken place detrimental to her position at Court. The powerful Andreades family, who had always been very well disposed towards her, had been asked to leave Brazil. Don Juan do Souza, her chief friend and adviser at Court, whom she was to contact immediately on arrival had died. This was to be a great loss.

Barely had her ship dropped anchor and the pilot come aboard, when she received the message that she was to proceed at once to San Cristovao, there to wait upon the Empress.

'But how surprised I was on arriving at the gate, to find the Emperor loitering about by himself, evidently for the purpose of seeing me, though he turned away shyly as if he did not mean to speak. He appeared as if just risen from his siesta, he had slippers on but no stockings, and a light gingham jacket and trousers, and a straw hat bound and tied with green; he was leaning with one hand stretched out to shake with me, as he said, "a moda Ingreza". I was very well satisfied with his reception of me.'

But the next encounter, with an extraordinary young man known as Placido, the Barber, was disagreeable to the extreme. This Figaro-like character, who made up in low cunning for the gay charm exercised by his operatic counterpart, reigned supreme over the imperial household. He combined the post of being Imperial Shaver and Head Valet to the Emperor with that of Head Housekeeper, Private Secretary and Director of the Kitchens. Placido hated his Austrian mistress, calling her 'The Stranger'. In time, he was to hate Maria Graham, the Englishwoman, as much. But on meeting her for the first time, he merely gave her a cool appraising glance, then escorted her silently to the small suite of rooms which lay directly off the wing occupied by the Empress and her children.

What Maria's rooms lacked in space, they made up for in the magnificent view from their windows. Below them, lay the lovely tropical garden with heavily scented, waxy flowers smothering the bushes. Tiny humming-birds and gorgeous butterflies, darted or fluttered along the winding shell-paths where hidden water bubbled and monkeys chattered. The high, crested green peak of the Beco do Perroquito dominated the distant sky-line.

With a sigh of relief, Maria noticed that the book-shelves she had asked for had not been forgotten. They lined the simple, white-plastered walls from floor to ceiling. Her slave, Black Anne, who had attended on her in Rio, had been re-engaged. At least, it was one familiar face amongst dozens unknown and expressionless. For into her rooms now, shuffling and whispering, came the Ladies of the Wardrobe to superintend her unpacking. They were all agog to see the elegant clothes, that the Imperial Governess must have brought from London. Were these the newest fashions? These simple, high-waisted gowns in Indian muslin and silk, so delicately coloured? They fingered the muslin. They stroked the silk. But they were not greatly impressed. Then there came a shrill peal of laughter. Black Anne was unrolling the modest camp bed in which Maria Graham always slept and which she carried about in a large portmanteau. Did she really sleep in that curious contraption, they asked? Only when her pair of enormous Carey globes appeared was her audience really impressed. There came shrill cries all round of, 'Marvellous! Marvellous!'

All the same, Maria recorded slyly in her journal, her simple chip-straw hat made fashion-news in Rio. It was copied in fifty different colours before the week was out and seen everywhere.

The day after her arrival, she was formally presented to her royal pupil by the Empress. At this introduction, a letter from the Emperor was read aloud. It gave the newly appointed governess 'absolute direction of everything concerning my Daughter's intellectual and physical welfare'.

This declaration was received in cold silence by Placido and his faction, particularly as the Empress naïvely showed her delight at such complete powers of authority vested in Maria, the Imperial Governess.

The following day, at seven sharp, Maria called upon the Princess, to discover the poor child being bathed, naked, in a kind of open apartment, in full view of the Empress's Guards as they patrolled the passage outside.

At once Maria gave orders that the Princess should take her bath in private. But her dressers refused to obey. Off went Maria to beard the Emperor. One can see her tall, slight, but determined figure, with her favourite gauze turban covering her head, striding through the passages of San Cristovao. As a well-bred Englishwoman, she was shocked at the primitive conditions in the royal nursery. She must change much, she realised.

Politely, the Emperor conceded to her first request, and she returned to face the indignant dressers. The Imperial Governess had triumphed. Little Dona Maria da Gloria was *not* bathed in public again. So Maria won the first round of a battle that had begun to rage secretly around the heiress to the Brazilian throne.

Later, Maria supervised her pupil's breakfast which consisted of a fowl stewed in greasy oil and reeking of garlic. Little Dona Maria tore at the bird with her fingers and then gulped down a glass of red wine. Her table manners were frightful.

Lessons followed. Alone at last with her pupil, Maria was able to present Mrs Barbauld's *Little Charles*. Seeing that the tale was printed in Portuguese and that she would be able to read it, Maria da Gloria was so delighted that she rushed headlong into her father's council chamber, to show him her wonderful present from England. From that moment, Maria could do what she liked with her royal pupil.

After morning lessons, came another heavy and quite un-
suitable meal, and then siesta; those hours of rest so sacred
to the Latin races, when the sprawling palace of San Cristovao
was sunk in sleep. Not a sound was heard; even the buzzing
flies on the walls had come to rest. The tiny jewelled humming-birds and exquisite butterflies haunting the garden, they
too slept. Alone in this palace of enchanted stillness, an
Englishwoman in a plain muslin dress remained awake, busily
attending to her correspondence.

When it grew cooler, Maria took the imperial children, a
trio of little girls, out into the garden. To their amazement,
they were told that they could run and play under the shady
palm-trees and yuccas. Mrs Graham was in the vanguard of
the new educational movement, sponsored by such enlightened writers as Miss Edgeworth and the Reverend John
Bennett, with whom she agreed implicitly how 'Attention to
a Garden is a truly feminine Amusement. If you mix it with a
taste for Botany and a knowledge of Plants, you will never
be in want of an excellent Restorative'.

She told her small princesses how little English girls were
encouraged to have plots of ground in which they dug and
grew flowers. Delighted, Dona Maria showed her a miniature
set of garden tools, given by her mother which she had not
been allowed to use. Her governess smiled, and told her to
use them now. No wonder the imperial children felt that
here was someone who understood their tastes at last.

After a third heavy meal called *bajo mao*, the Empress's
apartments were locked for the night. This ceremony took
place at sundown. Preparations began then for the night. In
every passage, small charcoal stoves were set up and round
their glowing embers, black slaves assembled their cooking
pots and baskets of fruit and food. All through the long slow
hours of tropic darkness, tasty little dishes were cooked for
the court ladies-in-waiting, who came out into the passages
to chat, eat, and gamble with Placido and his companions.
No one went to bed. In her apartments, poor Maria would try

to read or write by candle-light. But it was quite impossible to concentrate while that incessant chatter, punctuated with shrill peals of laughter, sounded at her very doors. The unpleasant smell of frying fat mixed with pungent garlic that percolated from every passage offended her delicate English nostrils. Sleep banished and work impossible, she would go and stand by her opened window. Here only was peace and coolness; the velvet blackness of the garden below was stabbed by sudden pinpoints of light from darting fire-flies while thick scents came up from hidden flowers. England seemed far away and her married life a dream that was no more. She was utterly alone in this strange theatrical palace of opulent splendour allied to primitive squalor where she could trust no one but the Empress. What would be the end? Would she succeed or fail as Imperial Governess?

Very soon she discovered that her royal pupil had no fit playmates of her own, only the slave children whom she was encouraged to pinch, smack and tyrannise over. Maria was shocked. Gently she tried to reason with Dona Maria. Princesses, Her Highness was told, must not behave as she did, for then 'they made a great number of people very unhappy'. In future, she must try to be more like her kind and considerate mother.

Maria was seeing more and more of the lonely Leopoldina. Every afternoon while the inhabitants of San Cristovao lay drugged in sleep, the two ladies would meet in the Empress's boudoir to discuss the latest books arrived from Europe, or to pursue their much-loved botanical studies. Their friendship was jealously noted, and the name by which the Empress addressed the governess. She called her – who was only a servant, after all – by the curious title of 'Madam'. The court ladies were annoyed still further by Madam, who entirely re-organised the routine observed in the Princess's private apartments. Placido and his favourites now found themselves barred from appearing every night in the passages to gamble and flirt with the ladies-in-waiting who were naturally furious.

Maria Graham, a portait by Thomas Lawrence

Miss May

In turn, the imperial governess's casual behaviour with the flirtatious Emperor whom they all adored, came in for heavy criticism. Everyone objected to the way she never kissed his hand or curtsied when he came into a room. She was called 'a heretic damnata' for this. One morning, in a mischievous mood, Maria swept the astonished Emperor a deep curtsey as he came into his daughter's room, and then, taking his hand, kissed it politely. He burst out laughing. In amused retaliation, he seized Maria's hand and shook it, crying loudly, 'This is the English custom of a morning!' Such informality infuriated every glowering lady present.

So the weeks passed by bringing endless small annoyances. Maria tried to overlook the spiteful behaviour of these childish court ladies, 'who spoke no language but their own, were illiterate, petty-minded and always busy in some political or domestic palace intrigue'. But it needed all her powers of self-control and much ingenuity to keep her temper and the peace. She soon came to be known as 'The Second Stranger'.

It is quite obvious, reading between the lines of the unpublished journal kept by Maria Graham when she was Imperial Governess, that the Emperor admired her courage and independent mind. The fact that she was a personal friend of Lord Cochrane, and of all the high-ranking English officials stationed in Brazil, had absolved her from appearing, by special permission, at the most boring of the many boring court functions. This privilege of hers rankled. Matters came to a head, suddenly, on the eve of the festivities organised for the Emperor's birthday in September. Maria had been aware of the angry mutters that always accompanied her entrance into the Princess's apartments. But now these mutters swelled into a mighty roar of questions hurled at her turbaned head. Did the Nursery Governess know that she must attend such an important function as the Birthday Court, 'dressed in the Court Livery of embroidered white satin, with a green satin train and white feathers, and to stand close to the Throne in case the Royal Child should require her handkerchief?' No, smiled Madam sweetly, she did not. And then, quite calmly, she went on to explain that she was not a court servant, bound by their laws, and she was *not* attending the Birthday Court. Amazed and furious, the court ladies determined to make Madam pay for what they called her foreign insolence.

First they set to work on poor little Dona Maria da Gloria and when Maria went to breakfast with her the following day, she found the child alone. No one had come near her, that morning, she said; no one had washed her or put on her pinafore. She was hungry, dirty and unkempt. Off went Maria, furious, to find the Empress. She met her in the passage outside, just come in from her early morning ride. She was still in her long, green habit and her eyes were red with weeping. In one hand, she held a single sheet of paper. It was from the Emperor. In his own handwriting, he confined Mrs Graham to her apartments except when the Princess's English lesson took place. This was the last straw. With her head erect and eyes flashing, Maria informed the shattered Empress that it had become quite impossible for her to continue her duties at San Cristovao so long as she was virtually treated as a State prisoner. Frankly, she told Leopoldina that her character was misunderstood and her services unappreciated by the Emperor and his Ministers.

Reluctantly, the Empress agreed; then, lowering her voice, she told Maria that her enemies were pressing the Emperor to dismiss the Imperial Governess, as they feared her growing influence.

Poor unhappy Leopoldina! It had always been her fate to part from those she loved best. Hastening into Maria's room, the two women concocted the following letter which the Empress was to hand immediately to the Emperor.

'SIRE,

It is with feelings that I cannot express that I receive the Order to-day, signed by your Imperial Majesty.

I should never have quitted England nor a family which is honourable, even in that distinguished country, to be a mere teacher of the English language! If I am not Governess of the Imperial Princess I have nothing to do in this Country. The person honoured with the title and employment of Governess in such a family ought to have been secured from the impertinences I have met with since I have been here. I will never submit to them. For my own sake I have no pride (*amour propre*) but for the sakes of my Pupils there was an absolute necessity for my not being treated as a servant. I earnestly beg your Majesty will give me leave to retire.

I shall quit Brazil, forever, by the first ship that sails.

Regretting my Pupils, regretting also that I have been unable to fulfil the wishes entertained by Your Majesty and the Empress when you invited me here as Governess.

As to those Ladies who have invented so many falsehoods concerning me, I forgive them and pray Your Majesty may never find reason to have listened, too eagerly, to their complaints.'

It only remained for the Empress to take this letter now to the Emperor. Back she came with his reply a few minutes later. The Emperor gave Mrs Graham permission to leave San Cristovao whenever she wished, and that 'most amiable lady' – as Maria usually described the Empress – was again in floods of tears.

Hoping to the last that her departure might be postponed somehow, Leopoldina helped her only friend, 'dear Madam', to pack. She begged the gift of some school-books so that her daughter could continue her studies with her. The two huge Carey globes she bought.

Pending the Imperial Governess's official departure, the whole court hummed with gossip. It came out that it was old Dona Maria da Cabral, chief attendant on the Princess, who had precipitated matters and was the root of all the trouble.

Pock-marked and flat-nosed, like some huge fat toad, whose jewel-bright eyes miss nothing, she had been fiendishly jealous of the tall, graceful Englishwoman from the start. For all her ugly looks, Dona Maria had the Emperor's ear. Disturbing His Majesty at that most sacred hour of all, the royal siesta, she had flung herself down by his bed, sobbing and crying. Was it fair to her or to other loyal palace servants that a complete stranger, whose power of speaking so many languages (that was the rub!) made it so easy for her to intrigue against them all, was upsetting their lives? 'The English Governess', she cried, 'tyrannises over the Heiress of the Most Noble House of Branganza and if she is allowed to continue this disgraceful behaviour, I, together with all the followers of the Imperial Family, will leave the Palace.'

It was an ultimatum. Besides, the infuriated old hag continued, was not His Royal Majesty aware that revolutionary ideas were being put into Dona Maria's little head? Constantly, the child was told that her royal blood was no different from anyone else's. She played in the garden now like any slave child; she even dug the ground. A frock had been torn; her pretty hands soiled. Once, she had heard the governess say that 'a Princess could make a great number of people unhappy!' What impertinence!

And so on and so forth. Longing to be free of this ugly disturber of his mid-day sleep, the Emperor rose and scribbled his note ordering Mrs Graham to be confined to her apartments outside lesson hours. But later, when Dona Maria da Cabral had disappeared, full of malicious glee, the Emperor began to repent of the hasty way he had dismissed the good-looking Englishwoman gracing his court in her plain muslin gowns and turbans. He admired her. Besides, she was most useful in taking his dull, blue-stocking wife off his hands and so allowing him more time to pursue his questionable amours. He had no doubt that she was training his eldest daughter to fulfil her high station, admirably. Her manners had improved greatly and wherever Mrs Graham was, there was order and peace instead of incessant quarrelling and confusion.

When the Emperor heard that Placido, over-excited by the news of Mrs Graham's impending departure, had refused to allow her the use of any royal carriage so that she would have to leave San Cristovao ignominiously on foot, he was so indignant that he placed his own coach at her disposal. He even hinted at a change of the imperial mind. Would Madam not reconsider her decision to go?

But Maria's wish to leave was final. On the 10th October 1824, with her camp bed folded back into her portmanteau and all her books packed, Maria Graham stepped into the Emperor's private coach, attended only by her maid, Black Anne. Holding a letter from the Empress in her hand she swept through the gates of San Cristovao for the last time. How many delighted, black, staring eyes watched her go? They were all there, I think, Placido and Dona Maria da Cabral, hiding behind the Palace windows, to see the last of the hated foreigner. Only one patient figure, one pair of weeping blue eyes sincerely mourned the departure of a remarkable Englishwoman who had been, for such a short but sweet time, her only friend and comforter.

This is the letter in which Leopoldina expressed her feelings at 'dear Madam's' departure and which Maria read in her carriage on her way back to Rio.

'My very dear Friend,

I have your amiable letter and believe me I have made a very great sacrifice in separating myself from you, but my destiny has always been to be obliged to estrange myself from those persons dearest to my heart and whom I esteem.

But be persuaded that neither the frightful distance which must in a short time separate us, nor the other circumstances which I foresee shall ever weaken the lively friendship and true esteem which I vow to you and of which I shall always anxiously endeavour to give you proof. I venture also to renew my offers to you. If I can be useful to you, you will contribute to my comfort by accepting them.

Again assuring you of all my friendship and esteem.

I am your affectionate friend,

MARIA LEOPOLDINA

San Cristovao – 10th October 1824

PS The packet of books have just been delivered to me and will be extremely useful to me in teaching my beloved Maria. The catalogue of shells which I send you will enable you, when in London, to procure me the kinds and species which are wanting in my collecton. I shall be glad to send you in return whatever may be curious or precious to illustrate the Natural History of Brazil.'

So the gentle Empress of Brazil and Maria Graham the Englishwoman, passed out of each other's life. Back in London, Maria resumed her literary life, reading for Murray and writing her own history of Spain, till her marriage to Augustus Wall Callcott, R A, took place on 20th February 1827.

Although much handicapped now by ill health, she entertained largely, became the adored centre of her new family, and finally wrote *Little Arthur's History of England* – a bestseller.

Till her premature death on 11th December 1826, the Empress Leopoldina kept in close touch with her 'dear Madam'. Her last letter to her, dated 22nd October 1825, is full of melancholy premonitions that she is about to die, in spite of the fact that she had just presented her still adored husband, the Emperor, with the son and heir he had long wanted. Maria is informed how well her ex-pupil is applying herself to her lessons – then, typically, Leopoldina asks 'dear Madam' for a Minerological Balance to be sent to her from England.

Though Maria Graham had failed in her post as Imperial Governess, she holds a unique position in that historic field covered by the activities of the English Governess abroad; for she was not only an enthusiastic pioneer but a born teacher at heart. When little Dona Maria da Gloria grew up and became Queen of Portugal in her own right, she paid Queen Victoria an official visit. As she drove through London's crowded streets of wildly cheering people, did she give a thought, I wonder, to that distinguished Englishwoman, who had first taught her how to live for others, and become a good Princess?

Three years after Maria Graham's death in 1842, the following advertisement appeared in *The Times*:

'Thursday, June 26th, 1845. Price with a supplement, 5d. Une Demoiselle Anglaise qui a recue la moitié de son education à Paris désire se Placer dans une famille en qualité de GOUVERNANTE. Elle ensegne des langues Francaise et Anglaise, la musique, le chant, et les principes du dessin. Elle préfère des jeunes élèves, et aime à vogager. S'addressera S.C., at J. Booth's stationer, 11, Frederick-place, Old Kent Road.'

From this advertisement, it can be deduced that the small stationer's shop is still acting as the governess's registry office. But the Old Kent Road? It seems an odd address for a high-class governess to advertise from in French? It was to Paris though, Paris of the Second Empire, that a young English governess who '*aime à voyager*' and taught music, singing, and the principles of drawing went in 1852. She went to be governess to the two daughters of the Comte de Tascher de la Pagerie, Grand Master of the Empress Eugénie's Household and her name was Anna Bicknell. Shrewd and sensible like Selina Trimmer, Anna Bicknell wrote a fascinating account of her governess life in the Tuileries, a vast gloomy palace with long corridors in which lamps flickered all day long and everyone was subjected to military discipline. Miss Bicknell spent her time rushing her two charges from one private class to another on foot as their mother, the Countess, thought continual carriage drives detrimental to their health. In the evenings, though, she presided over a tea-table set in her employer's huge drawing-room where she made tea, English fashion, and her pupils handed round the sugar and cream. Her tea-making, we are told, was much appreciated by such exalted visitors as Prince Chigi, the Papal Nuncio, and the Turkish Ambassador.

Anna Bicknell describes the Empress Eugénie whom she knew intimately, as a fascinating woman, but hard. She was far more drawn to the Emperor whom she describes as a very gentle and lovable little man. The Prince Imperial, a shy, lonely child, with large blue eyes and brown curls, had an English nanny. Miss Shaw was the perfect specimen of the nanny found in the best English homes and spent her time defending the Prince against the exuberant endearments and caresses showered on him by the Court Ladies whom she protested to Miss Bicknell 'were always worrying and frightening him' by their kisses.

Miss Bicknell was the essence of tact and whenever she played chess with the old Archbishop of Bourges who lived in the next flat to the de Taschers, she allowed the old man to win. He would say : 'I don't know how it is but I always get the better of Albion.' This was his pet name for Miss Bicknell.

In this way, she was a universal favourite. Court balls, banquets, intimate parties when only their Imperial Majesties were present – she took them all in her reliable British stride. Few governesses of her day could have been more popular.

The over-all portrait of the English governess abroad at this time follows the same sensible and kindly lines as Anna Bicknell's. Very rarely, if ever, does one come across our governesses hitting the headlines of the cheap press of their day like Mademoiselle Henriette Desportes, French governess in the Praslin family. In the summer of 1847, just before the publication of *Jane Eyre*, she was the central figure of a truly *'cause célèbre'*. Parisian newspaper-boys cried out her name along the boulevards while she paced behind the grim walls of the Conciergerie, a prisoner, with downcast eyes in nankeen dress and straw bonnet. A few days later, on 20th August to be exact, *The Times* came out with an editorial on *'l'affaire Praslin'*. Later still, the Duc de Praslin, with whom she was accused of being in love, died in the Luxembourg Prison of poison, self-administered, while waiting trial for the murder of his wife.

Henriette Desportes, as good as she was beautiful, was completely vindicated of the false accusation that she had incited her employer the Duc, to murder his wife. On her release from prison, she sailed for America where she married the Reverend Henry Field of the well-known Field family and became a notable figure in New England society. Her fascinating story has been told by her great niece, Rachel Field, in *All This and Heaven Too.*

Of course, there must have been many shady and queer English governesses at large on the Continent. Now and then we come across some curious advertisements in period French papers for a *'Gouvernante anglaise, méthodes drastiques'*. Such an insertion is open to much exciting speculation. But, they are rare. The honesty, deep piety, and, above all, unswerving devotion to duty of our genteel ladies dedicated to their profession wherever it took them, soon became a byword throughout the civilised world.

When the Second Empire came to a close with the tragic capture of the gentle Emperor at Sedan, Paris gave way to Imperial Vienna as the favourite European capital of English governesses. The Empress Elizabeth, born a Wittelsbach, commanded the Viennese social stage and as she was an ardent Anglophile, the demand for English governesses to teach well-bred Austrian girls increased enormously. They left England in shoals.

To mark Queen Victoria's Jubilee, a Home for Governesses was founded in Vienna in 1877 by the English residents. It was called the Queen Victoria Home for British Governesses and its first Directress was a Miss Bayle, who had been a governess herself. Under her régime, an incident took place at the Home which inspired Miss Elizabeth Kyle to write *The Skater's Waltz*, the title story of a collection of governess tales published in 1944. I am grateful to Miss Kyle for giving me the real story which she in turn, received first-hand from Mrs Krausse, an Englishwoman married to an Austrian, who served on the Committee of the Queen Victoria Home at the time.

It seems that Marie Vetsera's English governess, a Miss Crawford, was held responsible by the Vetsera family for having let her pupil escape from home on the fatal night when she joined the Crown Prince Rudolph at Mayerling. In consequence of this, an enquiry was held at the Governesses' Home to discover whether or not Miss Crawford had been guilty of professional negligence. Miss Crawford pleaded not guilty, her defence being that Marie Vetsera had asked her to accompany her to a fan-maker's shop on the night of her escape as a favourite fan of hers had been broken. On arriving at the fan-maker's, Marie had left Miss Crawford waiting outside for her in the carriage. Her governess did not know that the shop standing in a narrow little *Gasse* had two entrances; the front-one through which Marie ran in, laughing; the back-one through which she left in the Crown Prince's carriage driven by Bratfisch, his pet *Fiaker* driver, to keep her tragic appointment with destiny. Miss Crawford was exonerated and held free from all blame by the committee set up to judge her by the Home. When the question rose of her taking another post, the Vetseras decided not only to close Miss Crawford's mouth, tactfully, but to make her a belated *amende honorable*. She was offered, and accepted, a pension for life on the understanding that she left Vienna for good and never made her story public till everyone implicated in the tragedy had died or been forgotten.

Many years later, in 1915, a book appeared under the title of *Recollections of a Royal Governess* which reintroduced the Mayerling story. The authoress, who remained anonymous, was governess to the little Archduchess Elizabeth, only child of the late Crown Prince Rudolph and his much disliked wife, the Crown Princess Stephanie. Before this post, Miss May (May is the Christian name with which her letters home to her mother are signed) left England to be governess to the Countess Badeni whose husband was Governor of Galicia. She arrived at the remote Castle of Busk in Poland one dark autumnal evening in 1893, having lost her luggage en route. Unlike poor Agnes Grey who was left alone on arrival by horrid Mrs Bloomfield to wrestle with a plate of tough steak and cold potatoes in her mud-splashed dress and boots because her box had not been taken up to her room, Miss May equally tired and homesick was immediately made welcome by the Countess and her daughter, Wanda. A party was in full swing and the castle full of grand guests. In spite of Miss May's plea to be excused from appearing, downstairs, that evening, she was warmly invited to make her début in her dark-green travelling coat and skirt helped out by some exquisite pink roses presented by the Countess whose maid did her hair with as much care as if she had been her mistress. Miss May's first task was not to give Wanda lessons but to help her philanthropic mother, the Countess, cut out dozens of small yoke dresses with sleeves and skirt in one piece for the village children which the local nuns then sewed up. The Countess wished to introduce a more practical form of dress than the national Polish one. For weeks the good work went on: 'Oh, those yoke dresses I have cut! and still the good nuns, like Oliver Twist, are crying for more! The Countess got bales of stuff which was a most hideous mixture of red and black. The neighbourhood grew famous for these wretched dresses which were cut in three sizes like the bears of nursery lore, little, big, and middle size. All the little peasant girls were obliged to fit into one of the three sizes.'

Life was completely feudal at Busk, where wolves roared round the castle on winter nights and Miss May watched their lean dark shadows go flitting across the snow from her window. There were boar hunts and steeplechasing, endless balls, and strange religious feasts and ceremonies.

After a happy two years with the Badenis, followed by a short holiday in Italy, Miss May achieved her great ambition and wrote to her mother in England, 'You will be pleased to hear that I am appointed English governess to the Archduchess Elizabeth Marie, the only child of the late Archduke Rudolph, and granddaughter of the Emperor of Austria. I am delighted, as I always told you I meant to be in a royal family.'

On 1st September 1895, Miss May left Vienna for the Imperial Castle of Laxenburg, where she met the little Archduchess for the first time, playing in the garden, laid out on the lines of the Petit Trianon. She was a tall, fair, extremely pretty girl, very young for her age, with a passion for all animals, inherited from her grandmother, the Empress Elizabeth. After lunch they went rowing together on the lake and the Archduchess, being in great spirits now and less in awe of her new governess (she had disliked her predecessor intensely), began to splash her with water. 'I concluded that one of my duties was to sit and look pleasant, while I was being drenched. The kind of humour which consists in making people thoroughly wet and uncomfortable for one's amusement seems to be a brand peculiar to the upper sections of Eastern European society,' Miss May observed grimly in her book. The little Archduchess never splashed the royal governess again.

The following day on an afternoon walk the Archduchess found a young wild-cat nearly dead of cold and hunger. As she would not leave it, it was picked up and brought back to the castle.

'Our tea was waiting for us, arranged, as always, on separate silver trays. At once the Archduchess gave the cat all her cream, saying she would take half of mine. Of course the poor little thing lapped it up. Then, little by little, the Archduchess gave it my cream until none was left. This was an excellent opportunity for a moral lesson, so I told her if she gave the cream she must do without herself. That she must do without anything was an idea so new to her that it was fairly staggering. However, she agreed, and we gravely drank our tea, black.'

The education of a temperamental young Archduchess on English lines had begun. Miss May admits how, when she arrived at the Castle, she knew nothing of court etiquette or even what her duties entailed. But with complete self-possession she 'kissed the Archduchess's hands and made court curtsies as best it seemed to me. Not one of the ladies told me how to comport myself, nor showed me anything. However it did all right, and everyone said, *"You are so natural"*. I took it all as a matter of course and as if I had been used to it all my life.'

Again, British phlegm had triumphed. Rarely, if ever, do our governesses put a foot wrong abroad. Wherever they find themselves, it may be an imperial castle in the Tyrol or in a temple-palace in Bangkok, their absolute certainty that they are doing what is right to the best of their ability carries them through the trickiest situation.

The Imperial Austrian Court was reputed to be the most critical and scandalmongering in Europe; it was overbearingly stiff, too, and formal. But the little Archduchess was completely on the side of her English governess and taught her what to do at various ceremonies; how to curtsey and when only to bow. 'This for Grandpapa, this for Mamma, and this for me,' she would exclaim, delighted that she could be of use.

When the phrase 'waste not, want not' occurred once in a lesson, Miss May tried to explain what it meant to her pupil. But she could not understand.

'Later a roll of bread fell on the floor during tea, and I was going to pick it up. She said, 'Oh, it does not matter!' So I replied, 'But Archduchess, it is wrong to leave bread on the floor; some poor child might be glad of it.' She looked frowningly at me. She is of the same family as poor Marie Antoinette, and in this little Austrian Archduchess one sees displayed characteristics similar to those ascribed to that ill-fated Queen. I never understood Marie Antoinette so well before.'

'Erzsi' as her mother and Miss May called her, was soon reading *What Katy Did* in the best English schoolgirl tradition. She was introduced, too, to Sir Roger de Coverley, quadrilles and lancers, and *Pinafore*. In turn, the Archduchess put her governess to a severe test, by taking her out in her carriage drawn by a pair of Swedish ponies. Miss May had been warned that the child would do her best to frighten her but she must not pay any attention or show that she was nervous; if she did, her pupil would have nothing more to do with her.

'Therefore when she suddenly left the road and drove rapidly through the woods, missing trees by a hair's breadth, I sat calmly viewing the woodland beauties which surrounded us, apparently not seeing that out of the corners of her pretty eyes she was noting the effect; inwardly, I prayed a benign Providence which watches over children and fools to grant us protection. Of course, when the Archduchess found she could not frighten me, she gave up trying, and kept her pony carriage in its normal position, with the four wheels on the road.'

A governess of any other nationality would probably have screamed her head off and lost face forever. Miss May won her pupil's respect and love; so much so that one day she met her with this carefully rehearsed speech: "I feel sure that all archduchesses, princesses, duchesses, countesses and fräuleins" (this latter was meant to include me) "are all exactly the same." When I ventured to say that the difference was whether they were good or naughty, she cried, "That's just like you. You are never contented!" I had not realised what a tremendous compliment she had intended to pay me.'

In Vienna, Miss May had her own apartments in the Hofburg. She was the first imperial governess to achieve the singular honour of sleeping under the same roof as the Emperor. Like Anna Bicknell, in the Tuileries, Miss May found the Hofburg infested with soldiers so that it was impossible for her to move from one room to another without being under strict observation. In the Hofburg Miss May met Riedl, the Crown Prince's confidential valet, who had been with him on the night of the tragedy at Mayerling. From him, by tactful questioning, Miss May learnt what had actually taken place. She refutes the popular theory of a lovers' suicide-pact and hints that the Crown Prince was killed by one of his own entourage in a drunken brawl. Later, Marie Vetsera was shot whilst on her knees, praying, so that her mouth would be stopped. On her grave is a simple cross bearing the words, 'We come up as a flower, and are cut down'.

Every year on the anniversary of the Crown Prince's birthday, members of the Imperial Household rose early and dressed in deep mourning attended a 'Black Mass'. The little Archduchess, dressed in heavy black which she always opposed, made no attempt to read or say any prayer during the service. All Miss May could get out of her, was the sullen statement repeated annually, 'But it was not Papa I saw lying-in-state. Papa is not dead.'

The Empress Elizabeth visited her intense dislike of her dead son's wife on their child. She never saw her voluntarily or spoke to her when she did. One sunny afternoon in spring, while paying a visit to the Model Farm in the grounds of Schönbrunn and lingering on there till dusk, Miss May and her pupil were returning home down the Long Avenue when they saw a tall, slender figure, heavily veiled and dressed all in black, float more than walk towards them. In a panic, the small Archduchess clutched her governess by the arm, gasping 'Grandmamma!' Miss May was so startled, herself, by the apparition that she forgot to curtsey, even if she could have with the trembling Erzsi clinging to her. As the Empress passed them, wraith-like, Miss May heard a faint cold 'Good evening', breathed out more than said. Then she and Erzsi were alone again.

No wonder the highly emotional little Archduchess came to rely more and more on the calm, comforting presence of her tall English governess. Her mother, the Crown Princess, paid little attention to her; her handsome father was dead; her lovely Grandmamma an ice-cold legend. From her grandfather, the Emperor, she received the only affection she knew. He would come, quite alone, to see her and Miss May in the schoolroom. A simple, kindly old man to whom Miss May always spoke in French.

Almost the chief factor in the English governess's success with her pupils, particularly with those living in the supercharged atmosphere of a foreign court, was the stabilising influence she wielded in their private lives. She never intrigued, for instance, against their parents or participated in court politics or party intrigues; she never favoured one child more than another and dealt with each small culprit fairly. Above all, she brought a feeling of security and protection. With her orderly ways and neat dress, those rustling silk skirts and crisp blouses, that linen handkerchief smelling faintly of eau de Cologne, she was a most comforting presence. When Miss May found the appalling stiff rules and pompous traditions of the Imperial Court becoming too much for her, her British sense of humour nearly always came to the rescue. She was surrounded by jealous ladies of the Imperial Household, who would not accept their little Archduchess's love and admiration of her English governess. But Miss May won through unlike Maria Graham. She was still in charge of the impulsive and devoted Erzsi when, on 10th September 1898, the Austrian Court was shattered by the news of the Empress's murder at the hands of an assassin in Switzerland. Miss May was present at the ceremony of the 'Blessing of the Corpse' when with other members of the Imperial Household she gazed down through a small plate of glass let into the lid of the Empress's coffin. For the first time, she saw at close quarters, the beautiful features of the lonely and eccentric Empress who had always hated to be

Anna Leonowens

Emmeline Lott

stared at during her tragic life. Pityingly, Miss May comments how she was buried with all the pomp and ceremony shunned by her when alive in the great gloomy Hapsburg vault in the Church of the Capucine Friars; that loathsome tomb where her only adored son lay and by whose side she was placed.

Soon after the death of the Empress, the Archduchess was considered to be old enough to leave the schoolroom and her own suite of ladies-in-waiting were appointed. Packing her boxes, Miss May departed laden with presents from her Archduchess. Like Selina Trimmer, she had her own gold bracelet set with sapphires and diamonds, 'the handsomest piece of jewellry I have ever had'.

But one feels that she preferred the basket case that had been especially made to take her bicycle, handles and all, when she went travelling, together with a pretty leather bag, inset by a clock to dangle from the bars so that punctual, efficient Miss May could always see the time when she rode to keep her appointments. She was a great bicyclist and the first lady in Vienna to be seen riding in public, special permission having been granted to her from the Crown Princess. No doubt she carried on this practice in Rome where she went next to be governess to the Duchess of Bomargo's only daughter.

There were many English governesses abroad, contemporaries of Miss May, who might have told tales as strange as hers of Mayerling. To a ripe old age, they lived on in the draughty, ancient castles, belonging to the mid-European aristocracy. Seldom introduced to guests invited for the great boar-hunts, organised by their employers, and wearing old-fashioned garments of rusty black, they were often mistaken for poor relations. Though made to feel their social inferiority when Royalty was entertained, or the Burgomeister called, in private, they ruled their grown-up pupils with a rod of iron by sheer force of habit; more often than not, they were buried in the huge stone vaults of the family with whom they had become completely identified.

L

The Far East as well as Europe claimed the services of the English governess in the nineteenth century. Wealthy Indian Princes wished their children to speak English in preparation for the day when they were sent to the public schools and universities of the land ruled over by the great White Empress.

In Delibes' opera *Lakmé*, produced at the Opéra Comique, Paris, 1883, there appears the only operatic English governess on record. Typically, Miss Bentson thinks India 'an abominable country' and sings, true to character, in a rich contralto voice: 'When I think how comfortable we might be now in London, in Hyde Park, inhaling that delightful fog that gives us our clear complexions.'

She is always addressed as 'venerable Miss Bentson'.

It was in India, after the death of her young husband, an Indian Army Officer, that Anna Leonowens opened a small school for officers' children in 1859. It soon attracted the attention of Mr Tan Kim Ching, the Siamese Consul at Singapore, who had been instructed by the shrewd and enlightened King Mongkut of Siam to find an English governess for his numerous offspring. Mr Ching advised His Majesty to engage Mrs Leonowens and Anna received a curiously phrased letter, one day, formally inviting her to go to the Royal Palace at Bangkok, 'to do your best endeavour upon us and our children'.

Her best endeavour was to include teaching the English language, science, and literature. The letter was dated, English era, 1862, February 26 and signed S S P P, Mana Mongkut.

Anna Leonowens accepted this invitation and left Singapore for Bangkok with her small son, Louis, and two native servants.

On her arrival in Bangkok, Anna Leonowens discovered to her dismay that she was expected to live inside the Palace and conform to harem laws. She made her first stand, declaring to the infuriated King Mongkut that as an independent widowed Englishwoman, suitable accommodation for her son, her servants and herself must be found outside the

Palace. The King tried to force Anna to give in to his wishes but she was adamant. Finally, a small and very dirty house and garden on the river was handed over to her and the triumphant Mrs Leonowens moved in to face a major spring-cleaning.

Her schoolroom was in a temple – the Temple of the Mothers of the Free. A most appropriate name, for Mrs Leonowens was to bring freedom of ideas and a new approach to life to many of the royal wives and concubines as well as book-learning to their children. Every day, she walked through the long, dim corridors of the temple to her classroom accompanied by the low chant of distant prayers. Lessons began immediately after the Buddhists' morning service which she was obliged to attend to muster her pupils in good order after it. She taught between twenty and twenty-five princes and princesses of the blood royal besides several gentlewomen, and later wives of the harem. Her most remarkable pupil was Prince Chulalongkorn, the Heir Apparent whom she found 'modest, affectionate, eager to learn and easy to influence' and his young sister, the delicate and fairy-like Princess Fa Ying.

Lessons were conducted at a long, richly-gilt table strewn every day with offerings to the priests of Buddha. The bronze censers on it still smoked with fragrant incense when Mrs Leonowens sat down at the head of it and there were always tall gold vases filled with exotic flowers. The favourite studies of the royal Siamese children were geography and astronomy. But the only map they had ever seen and used had a great patch of red on it, and above a little one of green. In the centre was a figure cut out of silver paper which held a huge pitchfork in one hand and an orange in the other. This figure represented the King, while the big scarlet patch was Siam, the little green one Burma. On the north side of the green patch was painted a huge Englishman, sporting a cocked hat with red feathers, holding in his arms a large tract of land. This was Lord Clive, clasping British Burma.

'The rest of the map was all blue, and all round the Siamese territories richly painted and heavily freighted ships were sailing to and fro. But the poor Burmese monarch had not a boat to display. My simple pupils knew just so much as this map taught them and no more.'

Burma on the north, and Siam on the south, and the sea all round – this was the world to them.

'But of their celestial geography they could tell me a host of interesting particulars, all of which they would relate with the accuracy and picturesque vividness of a fairy-tale; and whenever a dispute arose as to the height of some of the mountains or the depth or breadth of the oceans in the celestial worlds, they would refer at once to a Siamese book called *Tri Loke Winit Chai* – a book which settles all questions about the three worlds, of angels, of demons, and of gods . . . .'

Naturally, when a proper English map and globes of the celestial and terrestial spheres arrived at Bangkok, they created quite a sensation in the temple schoolroom. For nine days, Anna Leonowens had her hands full, coping with the crowds of women who came from the royal harem to learn the wonders of modern geography and astronomy. They learnt to see Siam as a mere speck on the universal globe and were much consoled by the fact that England, Mem's country, occupied even a smaller space.

Unlike most Western children, Anna Leonowens found her Siamese pupils full of eager inquiries about the sun, moon, and stars. But they wished to have them peopled always by ghosts and hobgoblins. They could take a box of ice from Singapore as an object-lesson but snow – snow they simply could not believe in.

Even the serene and lovely Hidden Perfume, a wife long out of favour, came up to her dear Mem and laying her hand on her arm said: 'Please do not say that again. I believe you like my own heart in everything you have taught me, but this sounds like the story of a little child who wishes to say something more wonderful than anything was said before.'

From that moment her pupils would not believe her simplest statements and Anna had to go to King Mongkut and inform him of this new dilemma. He accompanied her back to the Temple and told the royal children and ladies of the harem that, 'It was just possible that there was such a thing as snow, for English books of travel spoke frequently of some phenomenon which they designated as "snow".'

After the King had spoken, there was no more trouble.

One morning as Mrs Leonowens' pupils were studying an ancient map of Egypt, tracing the source of the Nile, something fell from the vaulted roof overhead, down on to the chart spread on the table.

'It looked like a beautiful thick silk cord neatly rolled up; in another instant, however, the coil unrolled itself, and began to move slowly away. I screamed, and fled to the extreme end of the temple. But what was my surprise to see all my pupils sitting calmly in their seats, with their hands folded in veneration and their eyes fixed in glowing admiration on the serpent as it moved in tortuous curves along the entire length of the table. With a blush of shame and a sense of inferiority I returned to my seat and watched the beautiful creature; a certain feeling of fascination dawned upon me as I looked into its clear, bright, penetrating eyes; the upper part was of a fine violet colour, its sides covered with large scales of crimson edged with black; the abdominal parts were of a pale rose colour edged likewise with black; while the tail terminated in tints of bluish ash of singular delicacy and beauty. As the snake dragged itself slowly to the edge of the table I held my breath in terror, for it dropped on the arm of the chair in which Prince Somdetch Choufa Chulalongkorn (the Crown Prince) was seated, whence it fell on the floor, trailed itself along through the dim corridor and down the steps, and finally passed out of sight under the stone basement of the temple.'

Immediately the royal children jumped up from their seats and clustered round Anna Leonowens in the wildest joy, telling her that the gods, indeed, loved her and favoured her teaching. Hadn't the crimson-bellied sacred snake, Gnuthong-dang, appeared full of happy omens? The very fact that it had dropped on the arm of the Crown Prince's chair was an unmistakable sign that he would one day become famous in wisdom and knowledge. From that day, whatever Mem taught them was acceptable. She had her own private battles of course with the King but even he was forced to listen to this small, resolute young woman with the brown eyes and hair who upheld the cause of the humble, poor, and downtrodden; to whom his cruel despotism was hateful in every way and who never ceased to teach his son, the future King of Siam, that he must, above all things, be tolerant and grant freedom to his oppressed and enslaved people. When after five and a half years of arduous work, of continual arguing and pleading with King Mongkut, he is reported to have said to her:

'Mem, everyone is in affliction of your departure. Even that opium-eating secretary is very low down in his heart because you *will* go. It shall be because you must be a good and true lady. I am often angry on you and lose my temper, though I have a large respect for you. But nevertheless, you ought to know you are a difficult woman and more difficult than generally. But you will forget, and come back to my service, for I have more confidence on you every day. Goodbye.'

But Anna Leonowens, one of the most courageous and enlightened women of her day and a great governess, never returned to Siam though she left her mark forever in that country.

During the years that she was royal governess she completely revolutionised the lives of the King's chief wives and concubines by her teachings and so profoundly influenced the mind of Prince Chulalongkorn, the Heir Apparent, that during his reign slavery was abolished and many social reforms begun.

Anna Leonowens left Siam in the summer of 1867 and like Maria Graham took to writing. In 1870, she published her first book, *The English Governess at the Siamese Court*, followed three years later by *Siamese Harem Life*, now reprinted and from which my quotations are taken. Both Anna's books were a sensation. Thirty years after her departure from Bangkok, Anna Leonowens had a memorable meeting in London with her old pupil, the Crown Prince, now King Chula. He reminded his dear Mem of the promise he had once made to her, that he would rule over a free Siam. This he had accomplished. It had not been easy and there was much still to be overcome but the social reformation of his country had begun.

Till the last Anna Leonowens lived an active and independent life and died at the age of eighty-one in 1915. At this moment of writing, she has been made the glamorous heroine of a Hollywood film, *Anna and the King of Siam* and of a musical play, *The King and I*, which has had a phenomenal success on Broadway and has now been produced in London. Anna Leonowens, like Jane Eyre has achieved world stardom. What would she have thought of this, I wonder?

From her photograph, taken when she was seventy, from those deep-set, visionary eyes which faced a king's wrath so calmly, I feel that she would be interested, and not a little amused, by the limelight her work as a governess in Siam is receiving today. In the same way that Charlotte Brontë was interested and amused when she heard that *Jane Eyre* had been made into a play, and she confessed in a letter to Mr Williams, that, 'Yes, were it in my power, I should certainly make a point of being myself a witness of the exhibition. Could I go quietly and alone, I undoubtedly should go.'

In the same year that Anna Leonowens accepted King Mongkut's offer and became a royal governess, the Viceroy of Egypt's London agent engaged the services of Miss Emmeline Lott as governess to his royal master's only son and heir, the Infant Pasha. In her book *The English Governess in Egypt and Turkey* published in 1865, Emmeline makes a polite allusion of course to Lady Mary Wortley Montague and then continues:

'But it was reserved to a humble individual like myself, in my official capacity as Governess to His Highness the Grand Pasha Ibrahim, the infant son of H H Ismael Pasha, the Viceroy of Egypt, to become the unheard-of-instance in the annals of the Turkish Empire, of residing within the *foci* of intrigue, the Imperial and Viceregal Harems of Turkey and Egypt; and thus an opportunity had been afforded me of, Asmodeus-like, uplifting that impenetrable veil to accomplish which had hitherto baffled all the exertions of Eastern travellers.'

Emmeline, it can be seen, is a disciple of the Amanda Ros school of writing. Like her she has an excessively florid style and abounds in vitality. Her story begins with her arrival in Alexandria, when boarding a train for Cairo, she fell in with an intelligent fellow traveller – a Greek merchant, called Mr Xenos, who soon began to warn her of the terrible dangers that lay ahead of her as a governess in a harem. Did she realise that she was consigning herself, an independent and civilised English woman to a world of sordid vice and intrigues? She was probably unaware that Eastern ladies were chain-smokers of cigarettes and pipes impregnated by narcotic drugs and that all harem slaves and nurses were filthy in their habits and eunuchs insolent in their manners. Life in the strictest European convent was infinitely preferable to life in a harem, declared Mr Xenos.

Miss Emmeline Lott only smiled sweetly and continued on her way undeterred. Cairo reached, she was hurried, after one night at a hotel, into the house of Mr B, who was of Greek and Arab parentage. A close friend of the Viceroy, she was to stay with him till her rooms were ready at the harem. It appeared that the Infant Pasha had had another English governess before her, a Miss T, who had been dismissed for visiting another harem on one of her days off. This had annoyed the Viceroy who had accused Miss T of curiosity.

Emmeline spent a solitary life at Mr B's going out for an occasional carriage-drive, and reading or sewing. She was given Arab food which disgusted her, for meat was either dried up to a cinder and served on skewers, or swam in a lake of fat. To drink, there was only wine or coffee à la Turque, served in transparent china egg-cups. Fortunately, she thought Turkish coffee delicious.

A few days after her arrival, Mr B asked Miss Lott to step out onto his balcony and watch the viceregal party drive by. The little Prince, aged five, who was his father's only legitimate child and heir, was too busy eating bonbons to look up and smile as he drove by. But the Viceroy and Princess Epouse both favoured Miss Lott with a polite bow.

The next day, a Mr H H called to say that the Viceroy wished a clause to be inserted into Miss Lott's contract, binding her for three years' service and doubling her salary. She was informed the H H Ismael Pasha had a horror of his son being poisoned, so she must never let him out of her sight nor allow him to eat food that had not been previously tasted by the viceregal doctor. Her official title was to be 'the Cocana', but, by special arrangement, she was to be addressed always as 'Madam'. She was never to leave the harem without the Viceroy's permission. This was only a matter of form and leave would always be granted.

Emmeline refused to bind herself for more than two years, in case her health suffered, and it was arranged that she could resign her post at any time on producing a doctor's certificate.

After more weeks of dreary waiting she was taken by boat and landed on the stairs that led to the harem. This was a plain white building, E-shaped, which stood on the banks of the Nile. As the harem gates closed behind her with a rusty clang, Emmeline's heart sank; but once inside an inner courtyard she was fascinated by the sight of hundreds of slaves, busily unpacking bale after bale of gleaming velvets and coloured silks from Lyons; fine clear muslins and gay cotton prints from Manchester; ribbons and laces from Paris and London. There were silk stockings, too, by the score, and pipes of wine; elegant buttoned boots for tiny feet; pastel-coloured boxes of bonbons and Cashmere shawls. This rich merchandise was all 'for the use of the inmates of that vast conservatory of beauty which I was yet to meet', Emmeline wrote pompously.

Two little boy-eunuchs escorted her into the presence of the Chief Eunuch, known as Kislar Agaci or 'the Captain of the girls'. He was the real Guardian of the Mansion of Bliss.

Emmeline describes Kislar Agaci as being a very tall man with a tiny head like de Quincey's. He was a drug maniac and loved his food! She was introduced by him to the Lady Superintendent, who was about twenty-four years old and called Anina. Anina wore a pretty lavender-coloured satin paletot over a muslin dress, finely worked, with trousers to match. Into her turban was tucked a red rose and she was a mass of diamond rings and brooches. A pair of ugly, black, patent-leather boots completely spoilt her otherwise charming appearance. She led the new Cocana over a thick Brussels carpet, 'soft as the dewy moss of Virginia Water and the same colour', recorded the homesick Emmeline, and then, suddenly, she was in the presence of the Princess Epouse and her son.

The Princess, who was a dwarf with fine blue eyes, sat on a divan of dirty yellow satin. She sat doubled up, like a clasp-knife, wearing a muslin dress that was soiled and crumpled and she smoked incessantly. Beside her stood H H the Grand Pasha Ibrahim dressed as an officer of the Egyptian Infantry in miniature. A small silver box, exquisitely chased, and containing some verses printed from the Koran as a talisman, hung on a chain from his shoulder. His complexion was dark and his nose short but he was a tall boy for his age. On seeing the new governess, he gave a yell and buried his head in his mother's lap. The Princess Epouse laughed.

She was attended by a bevy of ugly ladies with their hair and nails dyed a fierce henna-red. Thick, gold, English hunting-watches were stuck into their waistbands.

Ceremoniously, the new Cocana was shown over the Princess Epouse's apartments. Next came a visit to her own room. It was a mere alcove, bare of all furniture except a single iron bed, painted green. Pieces of wood, like old broom-handles, were laid across it to support a pair of very thin cotton mattresses. There were no pillows, bolsters or sheets.

'I gazed at the accommodation assigned to me with surprise; and yet what could I have expected, as every apartment which I had passed through was totally destitute of everything that ought to have been placed therein?'

Emmeline had been accustomed to 'the elegant manner in which drawing-rooms of the nobility are set off with fauteuils, superb occasional chairs and recherché knicknacks'.

Obviously, she had been a governess in the best families.

When she began to unpack there came screams of laughter from the harem ladies who had crowded into her room. Her crinoline intrigued them and her black straw bonnet which they poked at, crying shrilly 'Beautiful! Beautiful!' in Turkish. Later, she was made to walk slowly up and down like a mannequin, to show how European ladies manipulated their monstrous swelling skirts. There were fresh peals of delighted laughter.

Lunch consisted of the usual small pieces of dried mutton, stuck on a silver skewer and burnt quite black. With this dish (khebab), a flat cake of Arab bread was served, so salty as to be quite uneatable. The inevitable cup of finest mocha concluded this delectable meal, accompanied by a cigarette made of the precious golden-leaf tobacco of Stamboul. It had been sent by the Princess Epouse as a special mark of favour to the new Cocana. Emmeline was not a smoker and so she refused the gift tactfully.

At six o'clock, Shaytan, the Prince's Ethiopian Head-Nurse, presented herself to the Cocana with the request that her pupil wished to go walking with her. Out they went, the little Pasha and his governess into the Palace Gardens, which were full of splashing fountains. In a shady corner, Emmeline noticed a strange collection of swings, designed like old-fashioned barouches. Fitted with handsome cushions, they could be set moving by machinery. 'Swinging is always a favourite pastime with the Orientals,' Emmeline comments *en passant*.

Ignoring the swings that belonged to his father, the little Pasha led his governess through the Viceroy's pavilion to the state-bedroom, complete with a life-size, white mechanical polar bear and a tiger-cat. But what surprised Emmeline even more than these odd toys of the Viceroy was the absence of slaves. With the Infant Pasha holding her hand, she might have been wandering through a fairy palace staffed by invisible servants.

This tour over, the last meal of the day was presented to the viceregal children, each child being attended by its own head nurse, who literally spoon-fed them. Finally, the Prince was elaborately undressed, bathed, and dressed again, for bed. With his numerous half-brothers and half-sisters, he was put to sleep on what Emmeline described as 'one full-swelling bed'. A colossal mattress was spread on the floor of the reception hall; then, down from the ceiling, there came billowing and fluttering, an enormous, bell-shaped mosquito net. Like a vast canopy, it hung over the vast communal bed on which, not only the viceregal children slept, but their slaves and nurses as well. A silver brazier burned throughout the night in a corner. To Emmeline, it was as if some huge gipsy-encampment had suddenly materialised before her astonished English eyes.

Sharp at ten, the Captain of the Girls locked the outer doors of the Abode of Bliss in the same ceremonial manner that Placido, the Barber, had locked the Empress of Brazil's apartments at San Cristovao. Only there was no gentle and erudite Leopoldina waiting to talk to Emmeline as she had once talked to her most 'amiable friend', Maria Graham. To her dismay, the new Cocana discovered that she was expected to have supper with Clara, the German laundry-maid, and the only other white woman, besides herself, in the harem.

This was the last straw. Fuming with rage at having to 'hobnob', as she called it, with a mere domestic, she retired to bed.

She was alone at last. Alone in the harem where the only person with whom she could communicate intelligibly was Teutonic Clara. Of what use were her languages, French, Italian, German and Greek? She could only make herself understood to the harem ladies by childish signs and movements. As she wondered how to make-shift for bed-linen, she heard the dull groan of heavy iron bolts and bars being driven into their sockets, followed by the sinister creak of turned keys.

'Those grating sounds startled me; I could not realise my position; I thought I must be the inmate of some prison in a foreign land and not a guest in a prince's palace . . .

'Then did I experience the worst of all loneliness. Wishing, however, to divert my mind as much as possible, I resolved to keep a diary. But how? Putting two of my largest square trunks upon one another, for a table, which I covered with my travelling rug, and for a chair laying my travelling cloak upon another box, and turning a large one upright, I placed it at the back to give me support; thus did I begin to jot down these incidents of my experience of harem life in Egypt.'

The following morning, Emmeline made an angry stand against cleaning her wretched room and doing her own laundry. She insisted on taking breakfast by herself. After this meal, she would join her royal pupil and visit the three royal wives with him, a ceremony which began each day for him.

At noon, the little Prince lunched and then amused himself with some English toys presented by Emmeline. As he played, one of the Viceroy's daughters by a favoured slave-girl, happened to annoy him. Immediately, he began to pinch and beat the poor child till blood poured down her face; then, putting his fingers inside her mouth, he tore at the flesh inside like an animal. This was too much for Emmeline's British blood. She rounded fiercely on the infant Prince and slapped him. His Highness burst into tears and stalked off.

A few minutes later, the whole harem was in an uproar. Turks and Egyptians have a horror of seeing anyone in tears, Emmeline discovered. The poor child who had been so cruelly mauled was made to kiss the Prince's coat-hem and then prostrate herself on the floor before him. Again, Emmeline objected pointing out to the Princess Epouse who had appeared that she was not to blame. The Princess merely laughed saying to her, '*Malesch, Madame, Malesch!*' (It does not matter).

But matter it did most strongly to Madame, with her strong sense of national justice. She continued to tick off H H as she called him, whenever he misbehaved and did not conform to her standards of princely behaviour. '*Fena Pasha*' (bad Pasha) she would cry shaking her finger at him, adding: '*Fena, fena!*' (naughty, naughty!).

'At that time I was fully impressed, fortunately with the sense of my own power, and the notion that, being an Englishwoman, no harm could happen to me. Had any danger menaced me from any of the attendants of His Highness, I felt assured that my own special Prince would have interfered on my behalf. I have since learned that had I been 'spirited away', which in all probability would have been my kismet, had not Allah protected me from the tricks and manners of a clique, it would have required a considerable amount of outward pressure in the highest quarter of a Circumlocution Office, to have roused official inquiry.'

The age-old tactics of our governesses are revealed once more. Believing that they were always in the right, few of them came to harm, and in their determination to see English disciplinary methods carried out, they nearly always triumphed. Before long, the Infant Pasha listened quietly to what Madam had to say and it was rumoured all over the harem that the Cocana could do as she liked with him.

But any attempt she made to organise a regular system of training her young Prince was frustrated by his irregular life. One day, she would receive an order from the Princess Epouse, to take her son out at 6 am; another, it would be as late as eleven before they set out. Once H H was in the gardens it was very difficult to lure him back to lessons. His slightest wish was law and every whim indulged.

'I drew up a scheme for his education, and endeavoured to obtain H H the Viceroy's sanction to its execution; but that Prince explained to me that he did not wish his son to be taught from books or toys, as he would pick up English quickly enough by being constantly with me; so that I abandoned all idea of educational training.'

Eventually, Emmeline sought counsel from Mr B, the Viceroy's agent, to whom she poured out all her woes. He listened attentively, hearing how much she disliked Arab food and what little furniture there was in her room. She complained that she was constantly sent out with the Prince in the glaring heat of the day and that the air in the harem was so impregnated with the fumes of opium that she suffered from a continual feeling of apathy which was frightening.

Mr B was a broken reed in regard to improving living conditions. And so, Emmeline continued her solitary existence in that queerly mixed company of black and white slaves, of lesser wives and concubines. Her head ached continually from their incessant chatter in Turkish, Nubian and Arabic dialects. Life in the harem she described was like 'Bedlam let loose and they all grimaced like monkeys from four o'clock in the morning till ten at night'.

When Shaytan, the Prince's head nurse, grew so jealous of her influence, that she attempted to poison her, Emmeline determined to consult the three Head Wives and have them solidly on her side. In this, she was successful and through the personal intervention of the Princess Epouse, the Cocana was supplied with a proper table, chairs, and a night commode, for her room, while H H the Viceroy sent her a case of claret, a chest of tea, and special soup from his table. His own doctor, the Hekim Bachi, was ordered to safeguard the Cocana's health and a carriage was placed at her disposal in which she took a daily airing with her pupil. It was not long before everyone in the harem began to appreciate the Cocana's European ways, openly. Hardly a day passed when Madame was not consulted about some domestic detail. In fact:

'They had all become so attached to me before I left for Constantinople that, from their Highnesses the Princesses down to the very *Mihtur* (sweeper), all treated me with the greatest kindness, attention, and respect, which enabled me to gain that insight into their sayings and doings.'

Unfortunately, Emmeline's health completely broke down during her stay at the Old Palace on the Bosphorus. After a severe attack of neuralgia, followed by fever, she fell into such a sickly state of inertness that:

'I felt no desire to move: no wish to go into the "outer world": that my voice nearly failed me, that my memory seemed to be passing away from me, and that all remembrance of my home, my dearest friends, my most intimate associations, seemed gradually but *surely* fading from my mind. The feeling I then experienced was that of Bottom, in Shakespeare's *A Midsummer Night's Dream*. "I have an exposition of sleep come upon me", was my constant thought ... An inward conviction gained more and more the upper hand in my mind, that some calamity was hanging, like the sword of Damocles, over my head ... A voice seemed to cry: "Arise, arise, or you are lost!" I resolved to quit the Old Palace at once. I did so, and returned to Alexandria.'

Almost immediately, she gave in her resignation on the plea of ill health. It was accepted and she left for England.

In her second book, *Nights in the Harem*, Emmeline hints dramatically of what might happen to some governesses seeking situations abroad, at a time when the White Slave traffic was flourishing. We are told of the evil machinations of a certain Madame Tedesco, who lived in the Via de la Scala in Florence, where she had established an agency under the direction of a disreputable subordinate.

'The business of this second disgrace to her sex was to advertise in foreign papers for English and French governesses, required by families of rank and fashion in various countries. When her unhappy victims were entrapped, under the pretence of being supplied with situations, with cool deliberation this person showed herself in her real light, as a mere *jellal*, or slave dealer, and absolutely sold the more prepossessing of these fair exotics to foreign nobles of wealth. When the poor fading flowers had ceased to adorn the conservatories of the Florentine villas, they were packed off, as mysteriously as smuggled wares to Egypt, to decorate the saloons of Signora Tedesco where Pashas, ministers, members of the diplomatic corps, merchants, and roués of all countries nightly congregated. Many of the choicer plants from this foul soil were transplanted into the palaces of Egyptian Princes; there they vegetated, sumptuously tended perhaps, but in such *durance* vile, that no intelligent friends or relatives ever reached them. Many were, many are still, walled-up in these retreats and will pass away to the tomb under conditions which no mortal dare seek to unveil.'

Fortunately Miss Emmeline Lott did not belong to this wretched class of duped English governess. She was too clever to be victimised by the wiles, however cunning, of any Signora Tedesco. Instead, by her writings, she revealed to the reading public of her day how extremely dangerous it was to be a governess in the Orient unless possessed of great courage and endurance.

Though Emmeline lacked Anna Leonowen's superior intellect, she has originality and her touch of honest vulgarity is likeable.

A complete contrast to her in every way, Miss Eagar was hand-picked by a member of our Royal Family to be Imperial Governess to the little daughters of that ill-fated Tsar, Nicholas II. Miss Eagar is as discreet and reserved as Emmeline was forthcoming and voluble. The pen she wields is pure Baedeker and she only gives us facts and more facts, unadulterated by the tiniest pinch of spicy romance in her book, *Six Years at the Russian Court*, published in 1906. Hers are brief notes to palace life. In her preface Miss Eagar strikes a warning note, informing her readers that:

'She will deal only with undiluted TRUTH for so much has been written regarding Russia and the Imperial Family and so little known of Court Life that it would be easy for me "to pile on the agony"; to represent the Emperor as a much-ridden man; to picture plots and counter-plots; or hidden bombs; but no such things occurred at the Russian Court, and I am a truthful person, and have not started forth to write fiction, but plain, unvarnished Truth.'

In 1899, Miss Eagar travelled to St Petersburg in charge of a mysterious white linen bag, bound with official red tape and decorated by crusty, diplomatic seals. This strange addition to her luggage had been handed to her when she changed trains in Berlin by a servant from the British Embassy and endeared her at once to me. But St Petersburg once reached, we hear no more of her intriguing parcel. Why a governess had been deputised to act as Queen's messenger remains a mystery.

On 2nd February Miss Eagar took up her official duties at the Winter Palace and was formally presented to the Empress. The handsomest lady she had ever seen. Her two pupils the Grand Duchess Olga, aged three, and the Grand Duchess Tatiana, aged one and a half, received her very prettily in transparent muslin dresses trimmed with rich Brussels lace.

She was shown the imperial nurseries over which she had complete control as the Empress wished her daughters to be brought up by English methods. She was delighted to find that the imperial schoolroom, a sunny large room, was decorated, 'in a simple blue English scheme. The walls were covered in a chintz patterned by cornflowers and there was a plain blue pile carpet to match.'

Barely, though, had Miss Eagar taken in her grandiose surroundings when she was whisked off to Tsarskoe Selo, the 'Tsar's Borough', with her little Grand Duchesses. Here, at the smaller of the two palaces, a low white house with a green roof, built in the Grecian style by the last Empress Catherine for her son, Alexander I, Miss Eagar and her charges settled down happily. The park was charming, being planted with every known variety of lilac, the favourite flower of the Empress Catherine. Each bush was pruned to look like a miniature bouquet, ranging in colour from palest mauve to darkest purple. In May, these sweet-smelling bushes became the haunt of hundreds of little brown nightingales who sang every night. Miss Eagar was enchanted. When Easter came, she watched with some nervousness the traditional arrival of two hundred eggs for the imperial nursery. Each egg had to be hand-coloured and the Grand Duchesses always helped in this entrancing ploy. But what with paint-splashed fingers and pinafores, Miss Eagar did not approve at all. We hear constantly of a great many elaborately staged festivals and gargantuan palace feasts but of lessons very little.

When special tutors were engaged for the Grand Duchess Olga, they were called 'Your Excellency', and bore the surprising rank of General. They wore military uniforms, but their caps, with a tiny button in front, were put on at a different angle from the caps of genuine army generals. Miss Eagar does not say what subjects were taught by these curious gentlemen.

From Tsarskoe Selo, the imperial children were moved in

May to Peterhof. This was the Summer Palace of the Tsars, built on the Gulf of Finland. Here the Empress's third child, another girl christened Marie, was born. She was known as 'The Amiable Baby' because of her good temper. At Peterhof, Miss Eagar was given her own separate villa. The little Grand Duchesses adored Peterhof where in white sailor dresses and flat straw hats held on by a tight band of elastic under the chin, they tumbled each other round the haycocks in the park that looked like small brown apple-dumplings to Miss Eagar. They rode their fat Shetland pony up and down the broad avenues; they played at being haymakers with tiny wooden rakes; they watched the mild-eyed cows being milked and collected dozens of smooth brown eggs in a basket. They played like English children secure and happy in their country home, and Miss Eagar was always at hand to mop up sudden tears with her handkerchief or dab arnica on a bruise.

There were few of Europe's crowned heads that Miss Eagar did not meet at the huge family gatherings continually taking place in one Grand Duchy or another. One month, the imperial children would be off by rail to Copenhagen to meet the royal Danish family; another, visiting Darmstadt where a vast concourse of Germanic uncles and aunts and cousins had foregathered. At these highly organised family functions, a bevy of royal English governesses were always present.

They remind one of a band of lady-gardeners called in to tend the most precious flowers. How assiduously they water the foreign soil in which they grow; how delicately they hoe and prune. But it is always a strong British stake they use, planting it firmly to insure the right kind of growth for the future. They know exactly when to encourage and cherish, when to curb and restrain, the tender plants in their care.

And so, while their royal nurselings played hide-and-seek round the rustic arbour of some Bavarian Schloss or ran races along the marble terrace of a gleaming white Balkan palace, a score or more of tightly-corsetted ladies sat primly upright on a garden seat, balancing a cup of tea in their hands. Good, strong, British tea made by themselves for once, and not by a flunkey, on a small methylated picnic kettle.

'Gipsy teas,' Miss Eagar called these European gatherings of the royal governess clans, where the gossip of one foreign court was exchanged for another. She is always discreet in the use of names. She hints only of this or that governess-personality. There is Miss W, so tactful and charming; Miss Z, rather a martinet.

So the years passed. One winter, Miss Eagar is busy reading *Alice in Wonderland* to Princess Olga, another, *Jack the Giant Killer*, to Princess Marie. She had no voice and could never sing in tune but her children loved to hear her rendering of 'Villikins and his Dinah'. Their favourite hymn was 'Rock of Ages', demanded at bedtime.

Special tutors come and go in the imperial schoolroom to teach subjects outside Miss Eagar's scope, but she always organised the making of all birthday and Christmas presents in the best English governess-tradition. One year a handkerchief-case was embroidered for the Empress; another, a kettle-holder for the Tsar. It had a small kettle and the words 'Polly put the kettle on', worked in blue cross-stitch. They were presents similar to those that English children have been making their parents for centuries. Though Miss Eagar doubted the suitability of a kettle-holder for such an exalted person as the Tsar of all the Russias, the Grand Duchesses insisted that their gentle, domesticated father would be delighted. And so he was, telling Miss Eagar that he would always use it.

On 12th August 1904 – Miss Eagar's birthday – the long-awaited heir was born. All Russia rejoiced. Unfortunately, the Tsarevitch's arrival precipitated Miss Eagar's departure from the Imperial Court. It was one thing to have an English governess influencing the young Grand Duchesses: quite another when it came to their future ruler, declared court officials.

Miss Eagar was granted a state pension of £100 a year and tactfully informed that her services were no longer required at St Petersburg. She returned to England, much grieved to leave 'the dear children whom I love so well'.

Her dear children continued to write to her in the careful, round, English hand which she had taught them. 'All the lilacs are out and the oaks quite green,' wrote Princess Olga, adding that Anastasia, the baby sister, 'had lunched yesterday with Papa, Mama and us as it was her birthday. She was good and ate very nicely and cleanly – How is your poor Mother?'

Like Hary-o Cavendish, Princess Olga knew exactly the kind of news her governess would most appreciate.

Miss Eagar had all their photographs, of course. Photographs in heavy silver frames. One showed her four, chubby, dark-haired little girls, sitting on a bench. They wore button boots with long, dark stockings. On their heads perched clumsy tricorne hats decked by an enormous pom-pom. When visitors came to call at the boarding-house that Miss Eagar had opened in Holland Park Gardens, these photographs would be handed round, together with the lovely presents given to her by the Tsar and Tsarina.

But the position of Imperial Governess at St Petersburg had had its drawbacks though Miss Eagar would never have admitted this. Miss Phair, who was a governess in St Petersburg at the same time as Miss Eagar, has told me what little personal freedom she enjoyed even during her time off. Whenever she left the Winter Palace she had to have police escort, being a marked figure. She was not allowed to join the English Governesses' Club Room, run in connection with the English Church at St Petersburg, or meet her countrywomen there on Sunday for tea. She was more or less isolated in magnificent splendour at the Winter Palace like Emmeline Lott at the Viceroy's harem in Cairo. This was the price paid for being a royal governess.

When the full horror of the Russian Revolution, followed

by the terrible tragedy at Ekaterinburg in June 1918, where the Imperial Family so mysteriously and tragically met their end, was made known in England, Miss Eagar must have been overwhelmed by the news. She was still alive but what had become of her dear girls, grown into slender creatures of deer-like grace, with small, proud heads? No one could tell her.

Her state pension came to an abrupt end; so, closing her boarding house in London, she retired to Ireland, where she died at Michelstown, having achieved the honour of being the last Imperial English Governess at the Court of St Petersburg.

With the elimination, then, of Imperial Russia after the Great War of 1914, followed by the gradual disintegration of Austria as a major European power, the field of work narrowed for the English governess. When Vienna was ruthlessly occupied by Hitler, many a shabby, coat-and-skirted English governess might have been seen sipping a *Kaffee mit Schlagzahne* in a once chic but now very much down-at-heel Kafe on the Ringstrasse.

For the aristocratic Austrian and Hungarian families who had employed them were either living in exile or had vanished into a concentration camp.

In England, with its educational system changing rapidly, the drift towards mass education had already begun. The private schoolroom was becoming a luxury that fewer and fewer parents could afford. Domestic and economic conditions were forcing the family governess out of her job. On the whole, girls preferred to go to boarding-schools, then on to college and the university. So the bell for old-time governesses, selfless and fond, began to toll, slowly, through the upper-class world. How fearfully the hearts of those on the last lap of their professional career must have beaten. They did not know, poor things, how they were going to make two ends meet when they retired in the new, embittered world of changed social standards and warring classes.

Before the knock-out blow came in 1939 to this dwindling army of elderly gentlewomen there remained one last stronghold for their traditional culture and old-fashioned respectability. This stronghold was Spain. Till the outbreak of the Civil War, Spanish girls of good family were brought up in nun-like seclusion at home. Their education was on strictly conventional lines and they each had a chaperone. With Queen Ena on the throne, the English Miss was as popular in Madrid as she had once been in Vienna during the reign of the lovely Empress Elizabeth. But the majority of our governesses in Spain were Irish, being nearly always convent-bred, and hailing from County Cork, Antrim, or Kildare. Many a Spanish grandee's daughter spoke English with a rich brogue, superimposed.

The English Miss had to conform to a strict code of social behaviour in Madrid, and even as late as 1924, she was not allowed to smoke or use make-up. She could not walk alone with a male escort. Neither could she go dancing in the most exclusive Madrid night club on her 'day off'.

On holiday with her charges at some chic plage, like San Sebastian, she had to wear her linen skirt unfashionably long and don a *traje de baño*, made of blue serge cut on voluminous lines.

In Miss Maura Laverty's novel, *None so Human*, published in 1944, the exclusive Miss Carmody, doyen of the English Governess Corps in Madrid, summed up the whole governess situation neatly:

'There was some reason for their discontent. Good food, a lovely home and an easy time did not make up for their lonely unnatural life. There was no social life for governesses, no parties, no dances. The English-speaking colony cold-shouldered them. Their aristocratic employers kept them in their places. They were living in the most romantic country in the world and they might well have been immured in a convent for all the male society they had. Not even the youngest and prettiest boasted a young man. Their only form of recreation was tea taken at a café or the monthly meeting of the children of Mary at the Reparadores Convent.'

Oh, those millions of cups of tea that have been drunk by English governesses not only in Spain but throughout the world for well over a hundred years. Cups of tea taken in moods of the deepest depression; in defiance; or in pure devilment whilst out with the forbidden boy-friend.

The English governess in Spain often spoke of 'going home' but by the time her fare was saved and her plans laid the damage had been done. She went on talking of a departure that never materialised. Her sedentary life combined with the luxury of a wealthy Spanish home had sapped what was left of her native pride and vitality. Pure inertia set in. She remained sitting in the sun, talking of what she might do *mañana*. When too old for regular work, many governesses gave English lessons or hired themselves out as duennas for a special occasion.

Very few of them achieved marriage with a Spaniard. On the other hand, quite a number of enterprising Irish governesses who were in Madrid before the Civil War broke out, deserted governessing for commercial business. They learnt to type and do shorthand and being bright girls, trustworthy and keen, many important Spanish business houses opened their doors wide to receive them. They could earn as much as 600 pesetas a month, while as governesses their wages were only round about 150 to 300 pesetas a month. What was more important, they kept their individual freedom.

But there was one remarkable Scotch girl who married a Spaniard and an Ambassador, at that, and became a royal governess. Her name was Fanny Inglis and her father was a descendant of the Earls of Buchan. Having lost his money at the beginning of the nineteenth century, Mr Inglis went to live in Normandy with his family, where Fanny learnt to speak excellent French. After Mr Inglis's death, his widow migrated to America with her daughters and opened a school for young ladies at Boston. Fanny taught with the rest of her sisters till her marriage with His Excellency Don Calderon de la Barca, the Spanish Ambassador. Soon after this event, he was posted to Mexico and took the charming, gay, and witty Fanny with him. She made a splendid ambassadress and a detailed account of her residence in Mexico, written in the form of letters home, was published by Chapman & Hall in 1843 under the title of *Life in Mexico*. The preface was written by Prescott, the historian, and it rapidly became a best seller.

It is a colourful and fascinating travel book similar to Maria Graham's *Journals of her Residence in Chile and Brazil* but far more imaginative in style and treatment. Fanny's descriptions of the Mexican scene are exquisite. One reads on, delighted, intrigued, and absorbed. She missed nothing and had splendid opportunities as ambassador's wife for observing all facets of Mexican domestic life, at close quarters.

On returning to the Court of Madrid, she was appointed royal governess to Queen Isabella's children. Queen Isabella had ascended the Spanish throne at the age of three. Throughout her reign there was great political unrest and eventually the house of Bourbon fell. Fanny Calderon de la Barca went into exile with her Infantas but when the Bourbons returned to power, she was created a marchioness. It is said that she always preserved an indomitable front to all warring factions and refused to be coerced into joining any political party. Her pupils came first. Social to the last, she died in the Escurial at the age of eighty-one of a cold caught at a dinner-party.

From South America, linked to Spain through historical associations, comes one of the most affectionate tributes ever made by a pupil to her English governess. In her *Testimonios* (Segunda Serie) Doña Victoria Ocampo, the well-known writer and editor of her famous journal, *Sur*, tells us how into her schoolroom, 'England arrived every morning at ten, with an immaculate blouse smelling of lavender. She

knew a lot of Nursery Rhymes which I rather fancied.'
England was Miss Ellis, her governess, who thought Vicky
Ocampo rather 'a wild pony'.

Whenever she misbehaved, Miss Ellis would take her hand
and patting it, say:

> ' Pat-a-cake, pat-a-cake, Baker's man,
> So I will, Master, as fast as I can,
> Pat it, and prick it, and mark it with V,
> And put it in the oven for Vicky and me.'

Immediately, Vicky would become as good as gold. She had
succumbed to the spell of our nursery rhymes with their
peculiar word-magic, and to the touch of an understanding
hand, in the same way that little Dona Maria da Gloria had
once succumbed to Mrs Barbauld's *Little Charles* and Maria
Graham's sweet smile.

So victory was scored, Doña Victoria Ocampo tells us, on
an ink-stained table covered by a shabby oilcloth on which
lay, higgledy-piggledy, smudgy copy-books, pencils and a
Graphic Reader bound in scarlet cloth. Doña Victoria, who
is a firm believer today in the English way of life, goes so
far as to say that she attributes her first attempts to become
a writer at all to her governess.

'One day I was feeling so injured about some punishment
inflicted upon me that I wrote an article in English against
the British Empire. Miss Ellis never saw it, though she
inspired it. I was ten years old and it was my first essay or
pamphlet; and that is why I owe to her the beginning of my
literary career.'

Although Miss Ellis used to sigh and tell Vicky Ocampo
that she never would be a lady, she knew just how to mingle
the useful with the sweet. Miss Ellis's method was to give
butterscotch as a kind of *douceur* while teaching history. She
gave the Ocampo children crackers, too, at Christmas and
made them a plum-pudding to give them added strength to
assimilate the dates of Hastings, Bannockburn and Trafalgar.

'The whole of English History, with its kings and battles, tasted of butterscotch and plum-pudding to me. It all seemed a jumble of dates, battles, and kings busy in having heads chopped off for them. Miss Ellis said they were nevertheless great Kings. And when she had done telling us about their tiresome greatness she always used to say, "However, he died." That at least was comforting news.'

While Miss Ellis was coping with the education of a future Argentine writer, another governess, Miss Edith Davison was bringing up a Hungarian-Croatian musical genius in embryo.

Early in 1900, Miss Davison went to Budapest to be governess in the well-known Pejacsevich family. On her arrival, she was met by the Count, her employer, who told her that her pupil, Dora Pejacsevich had not yet come in from her walk. Miss Davison must be prepared, said the Count with a gay twinkle in his eye, to meet a very dark little girl who had fallen into an ink-pot early in life. She would be carrying a bird-cage. Much to Miss Davison's amusement the Count's description of his daughter was exactly right. Very soon, though, her shy and very reserved pupil was calling her 'DIDI', and 'DIDI' Miss Davison remained for twenty-five years.

In 1904, the Count was appointed Banus (Governor) of Croatia and the family left for the Banal Palais at Zagreb, which was to be their home for the next four years.

From the Countess, who was a fine amateur singer and pianist, her daughter had inherited musical gifts to a marked degree. At twelve, she began to compose seriously.

In 1908, The Count resigned his governorship of Croatia and Miss Davison went to live with the Pejacseviches at their home, the lovely castle of Nasice in Slavonai. But every winter she accompanied her pupil to Dresden where Dora Pejacsevich worked hard at the *Konservatorium*. When the Countess was obliged to retire to a sanatorium on account of her ill health, Miss Davison supervised the running of Schloss Nasice till war broke out in 1914. Like hundreds of other English governesses, living with aristocratic families in Austria and Hungary, Miss Davison remained free to do Red Cross work. By this time Dora Pejacsevich's compositions were being performed everywhere, and her name was well-known. She was the first of her countrywomen to write a symphony that was received as an outstanding work in Vienna. Its first performance was given under the direction of the famous conductor Oscar Nedbal.

As soon as peace was declared in November 1918, revolt broke out in Hungary and Croatia. These were the days of Bela Kun and his Death Train. At Schloss Nasice, Miss Davison found herself in the thick of peasant risings staged by members of the 'Lelene Kader' (Green Squadron), who were really army deserters leading a nomad life in the great pine forests, burning ricks and plundering villages.

One night, the whole Pejacsevich family, including the young Count Pejacsevich's children, Miss Davison, nurses and the castle chaplain, a charming old Abbé, had to fly from the castle. They took refuge in a farmhouse. On the following day, they packed themselves into some wooden carts and set out in the pouring rain, each grown-up hugging a sleepy child, to try and stop the train bound for Budapest and safety. This they managed to do, scrambling into the luggage van as the train was already crammed full with refugees. Continually being shot at and crawling along at a snail's pace, their train eventually reached Budapest. But conditions were not much better here. In time, though, life became normal again and the Pejacseviches were able to return to Schloss Nasice. They found many of its farms in ruin and a vast part of the land confiscated.

Brilliant Dora Pejacsevich married now and offered her beloved governess a permanent home. But Miss Davison decided that the young couple were better left setting-up house without her. So she went to Zagreb, where she gave English lessons. There was a strong pro-British element in

Zagreb at this time which made her work a delight, she told me. Besides, many interesting personalities came and went through the town with whom she had contact. The outbreak of the Second World War found her again far away from England.

For a while, Edith Davison remained unmolested, but, one day, police detectives came to her flat and ransacked her desk and cupboards. After removing many of her private papers, they asked her to go with them to Police Head-quarters. A mild form of examination followed and then she was led down a gloomy corridor and put, for the first time in her life, behind iron bars. Her troubles had begun, to-gether with hundreds of other elderly Englishwomen living abroad in similar circumstances.

It was Easter Day when Miss Davison found herself locked into a cell which was already occupied by a solitary female. To her delighted surprise, she was one of her own pupils; a talented young Jewess. Two days later, after a brief talk with a high-ranking German Army officer, Edith Davison was sent back to her flat with her handbag intact to find all her private papers had vanished.

A few months of comparative peace followed; then the Nazis marched into Zagreb properly. Early next morning, every Britisher in the town was rounded up and put into prison except Miss Davison, who was taken to Schloss Nasice in charge of a special detective. In the very castle where she had been a governess for twenty-five years, she now found herself interned for the duration. The young Count Pejacse-vich had made himself responsible for her, so long as she stayed at Nasice. Ten days later, she was joined by other Englishwomen internees. After reporting once a day to the village police station they were free to do as they pleased. Time passed and the war developed. Now there came the Ustaasa Troops pillaging and burning Croatian villages. In Schloss Nasice, the English internees waited. What would happen to them in the face of this new menace? Instead of fire and rape and sudden death, that they had envisaged, there came a highly-efficient Nazi division. In Miss Davison's own words:

'We had greatly feared the German invasion, of course, but, although the German Staff was located in our house, we were not in any way molested. It reads rather like a comedy that the same vast buildings should house both the British Internment Camp and the German General Staff.'

In the huge pine forests that rose solidly green like a sea of petrified water round the Castle grounds, both the Partisans (Marshall Tito's troops) and the Ustaasa were operating fiercely. So Nasice was continually under fire from one quarter or another. One night, the castle was attacked and badly plundered; enormous quantities of food, clothing and bedding were taken.

'It was a terrible night,' said Miss Davison, who in company with the other British internees, had been sent to sleep at the smaller Schloss belonging to the young Count. 'But on the whole, the partisans behaved well and only asked us for food and cigarettes.'

After this nocturnal attack, the castle servants refused to stay any longer at night, preferring to sleep in their own village homes. The interned British left and Miss Davison remained alone with the German High Staff. Still under the Count's protection, she decided to stay at Nasice 'as long as possible, taking all risks as I had nowhere else to go'. There came a lull and then the partisans launched another and fiercer attack. Every servant fled. Miss Davison with a dog for her sole companion took refuge in the castle cellars. She remained in them for eight long days and nights, while an infernal racket raged over her head for hours on end. It was dark; it was cold; and it was very lonely. She had very little to eat and her poor dog, lying at her feet, trembled in terror at the appalling noise above them. Now and then, during a lull from firing, she would steal up the cellar steps and visit the military kitchens to beg a bone for her dog.

On one of these furtive sallies, she met with a deathly silence. The entire Castle of Nasice was deserted. The German division that had been quartered in it had moved away and Miss Davison was left alone, with the dead.

After another week had gone by, the maids turned up as usual from the village. They were delighted to find Miss Davison and her dog still alive and unharmed.

When another German Staff appeared, to replace the one which had left, Miss Davison was ordered to leave the castle. Some kind Croatian neighbours took her in and she remained with them till the end of the war. She returned to Zagreb in the autumn of 1945 and was repatriated to England in March 1946. She arrived almost destitute, after a period of over forty years' professional service abroad, and lives now in Scotland.

But there were many other English governesses, caught in the tragic maelstrom of total war, who were not so fortunate as Miss Davison. Old and feeble, they were herded into internment camps; others died beside the noble families from whom they refused to be parted after long years of service. I have heard moving stories of how some heroic English governesses ordered their ex-pupils to hide with their children while they faced, alone, the armed figures pouring up the drive of some remotely situated castle in Poland and Czechoslovakia. It did not matter whether they were Russians or Nazis, a guerilla band or merely some ferocious peasants determined to pay off old scores. Death was abroad.

On a few occasions these gallant old Englishwomen did manage to bring a savage horde of undisciplined men to a shuffling standstill by their extraordinary foolhardy behaviour. They literally mesmerised them to return from where they came by their superb indifference to the touch of cold steel on their cheeks or simply by the proud cry that they were British. More often than not, of course, their heroic bluff was called and they were killed with the aristocratic family they had tried to protect to the last.

Other English governesses, who managed to survive the gruelling war years in Nazi-occupied Europe were washed up as part of the most pathetic, human flotsam the world has seen. As far away as India they materialised, gaunt, pale Englishwomen, who had won through after years of appalling captivity. With all their savings lost, they faced repatriation to the country they could barely remember and whose language they spoke with an accent.

There is another aspect, too, of the rôle played by the English governess abroad in this last and most dramatic chapter of her history. It is a unique rôle which she could not possibly have visualised in her wildest dreams, nor could St Jerome, or any other idealistic planner of her professional life, have legislated for it either. Our parents were *au fait* with the beautiful lady spy who used to wheedle State secrets from handsome ministers and swaggering army generals over a glass of champagne in a discreet *apartement à deux*. But in our day these glorious creatures of a William le Queux thriller have been transformed into agents, looking like everyone else. When the War came, what was more natural than for a humdrum governess to step into their secret ranks? Again and again, the English governess abroad was found working in the underground 'resistance' movements that undermined Hitler's whole European front.

Of this distinguished band, was Miss Jane Walker, who saved the lives of countless escaping P O Ws in Warsaw. Originally, Miss Walker had been governess-companion to the two eldest daughters of the Archduke Ferdinand of Austria. Another 'agent-governess' was discovered by a young British officer when he was parachuted into Jugoslavia. On landing he was instructed by the local guerillas to contact an English lady living in hiding in a cave in the hills who would give him orders and a cup of tea.

Far away in the old Georgian city of Tiflis that lies on the Caspian Sea, Miss Mary Fellows did not have the opportunity to help escaping Englishmen or invite a gallant parachutist to tea. But in her own way she made her contribution to the war effort. Her simple act so quietly carried out epitomises, I think, what the gallant spirit and absolute integrity of the English governess has stood for abroad.

Mary Fellows was born at Aylesbury in 1868 and received an elementary education. Very early, while still in her teens, she was bitten by the longing to travel and went out to India to take up the post of nursery-governess in the family of General Sir James Browne.

In 1897, she returned home and began to study French, still an ace-language in the equipment of the best governesses. Three years later, she left England to be a governess in France, where she stayed for the next ten years, living mostly at Tours but visiting Paris and Rome. For her holiday, she would come home to take a Polytechnic course in languages till she won a first-class diploma in French. Next she began to study German.

Early in 1911, she left France suddenly for Russia and was never seen again by her family. Letters came at irregular intervals. But they told little of what she was doing or where she lived. On the outbreak of the First World War in 1914, they stopped altogether.

Years later in 1937, Brigadier Fitzroy Maclean, then a young military attaché, found Mary Fellows living in Tiflis, and put her into his fascinating book, *Eastern Approaches*. Arriving in Tiflis, he was told of a British war cemetery where some of our soldiers had been buried at the end of the First World War. But no one could tell him how to find it.

At last, a young secretary at the Municipal Soviet Office, advised him to try the NKVD. They gave him the address of an elderly Englishwoman who knew all about the British war cemetery. An Englishwoman in Tiflis! Fitzroy Maclean could hardly believe his ears.

Visiting the address he had been given, he found himself in an ancient courtyard before a large tumble-down house that had obviously seen better days.

It stood in the old-fashioned quarter of Tiflis and its carved wooden balconies were festooned by washing, hung out to dry. A small grubby boy was playing in the yard. As Maclean wondered what to do next, a voice came echoing down from the top balcony. 'Come up at once, Tommy,' it said, 'It's time you were in bed.'

It was the voice of England he heard calling; that cool, clear, authoritative voice, unmistakably embodying law and order. No wonder, the small grubby boy beside him stopped playing, and, straightening his back, called back in perfect English. 'I'm coming, Miss Fellows, this minute.'

Very much intrigued Fitzroy Maclean followed Tommy up the wooden, creaking stairs and so met Miss Fellows.

'She was small, white-haired and alert,' he told me, 'rather like a Scotch terrier.' One knows the breed.

She was with the same Russian family, that had first engaged her in 1912 and Tommy was the son of her original pupil. Triumphantly, Mary Fellows had survived the grim horror of the First World War and the Bolshevik Revolution when she had fled with her employers from St Petersburg to Tiflis.

Once her aristocratic employers had owned the whole house with its carved balconies and ancient courtyard; now they lived in a single room. Mary Fellows spoke Russian fluently but with a strong British accent and she told Fitzroy Maclean that he was the first Englishman she had seen for years. When he asked her if she had had trouble with the local Soviet authorities, she replied:

'None to speak of! They keep trying to make me give up my English nationality but I tell them not to be so silly.'

What answer could there be to such a superb statement of fact by an old governess?

Mary Fellows took Fitzroy Maclean to the little cemetery which she had battled for years to keep tidy and free of weeds. But what with stray cats and dogs and scratching hens, it didn't look as nice as she would have liked, she said, sighing deeply. This had been her own war effort, then, exiled far away in Tiflis. One can see her small, brisk but steadily ageing figure keeping its weekly tryst with her country's heroic dead. What had been her thoughts, I wonder, as she pulled at rank-smelling henbane or shooed away those mangy cats that would follow her? Did she know that her youngest surviving brother had gone to live in the north of England? If so, did she ever think that it might be nice to visit him? But how could she return to England when those silly Soviet officials had frozen her few savings in Tiflis? Besides there was Tommy who still needed her. He would always come first.

When Fitzroy Maclean left Tiflis, he asked Miss Fellows if there was anything he could do for her. But all she wanted was a wall built round her dearest possession, the cemetery, and this he could not do. He might leave her a few English books if he liked, otherwise 'she could manage perfectly', she said.

So Fitzroy Maclean left the little, white-haired governess who had reminded him of a Scotch terrier, to look after her graveyard and to see that Tommy, her pupil, went to bed at the proper time every night. Did she get her cemetery wall built finally? Has Tommy grown up into a nice-minded Georgian Anglophile?

On 7th February 1941, Mary Fellows died at the age of seventy-eight. She died in harness as she would have wished. Her youngest brother to whom I am indebted for the few, personal details of her long and obscure life, was notified by the Soviet authorities after they became our allies, of her death. Her savings, they said, had to remain in Tiflis or had she left them, perhaps, to Tommy?

All that remains to us today of Mary Fellows is that summons of hers, 'It's time you were in bed, Tommy'.

Like a triumphant clarion call it rings out over the whole civilised world, while behind it, echo other voices equally authoritative and clear. There is Maria Graham's from Rio

telling little Dona da Gloria at the beginning of the nineteenth century how 'a Princess can make a great number of
people very unhappy'. There is Emmeline Lott's insisting on
fair play and nursery justice from her cruel and jealous
Infant Prince Pasha. There is Anna Leonowens, reasoning
with her pupil, Prince Chula, how in the sight of God all
men, be they white, black or yellow, are free.

There are other voices, too thin now and far-distant, for
human ears to catch, which have told children all over the
world for a hundred years and more to clean their teeth
regularly and to wash behind the ears; to read both Shakespeare and *The Wind in the Willows*, not to cheat at racing
demon and to play a losing game always with grace and
good humour. From India and most European countries of
today, especially those behind the Iron Curtain, these voices
have grown so faint that they exist only as ghost voices in
our imagination. For a great tradition is dead. By the end of
this century there will be few children abroad – even fewer
in this country – who will be able to say proudly: 'Yes, I
had a governess. An English governess whom I loved.'

The Governess Today

The once sadly misused Victorian governess wheel has come triumphantly round full circle. The twentieth century governess with her college and university training is well equipped to enter any schoolroom, royal or common. She is a cheerful young woman, good at books and games, who is often asked to drive the family car. She makes a welcome fourth at bridge and even on occasions arranges the flowers. If, since the war, she says that she can cook and proceeds to help her harassed employer, struggling to cope with the children's lunch in a servantless kitchen, her value is, indeed, far above that of diamonds or rubies.

In a recent advertisement in *The Times*, no governess was asked to apply for the post in question, who had an aversion to flying, as she must be prepared to travel long distances by air. What more up-to-date qualification could be asked in a governess than to be air-minded?

But where are the young governesses, who are to take up their featherweight luggage and fly by BOAC or American Clipper to the utmost ends of the earth to which their historic forbears went so bravely but so laboriously by sailing ship or stage coach?

The visit I paid to the Governess Benevolent Institute in Victoria Street, London, bore out the truth of the sad story I had heard that the governess profession is dying. As the older generation of governesses retires, the ever-thinning ranks close up. For there are few fresh recruits. The pattern of English domestic life has changed utterly in the last forty years, and a revolution taken place in the British home which is as formidable and far-reaching in its social implications as the political revolution now convulsing the World. Economic conditions, such as the lack of servants, the housing problem in large towns, and the general lowering of incomes in all classes, has combined to make the private governess a luxury which few parents can afford these days.

When a 'country-house' governess is found, she is teaching, not one favoured pupil, but a group of girls recruited from the neighbourhood. Her activities are best described, I think, by this insertion which appeared in the Personal Column of *The Times*:

'Girls prepared with own daughter for School Certificate in lovely peaceful North-Country home; first class governess with many school certificate successes in charge; visiting Masters for Music, Singing and Drawing. Own bathing-beach, squash and tennis courts; excellent cooking; home produce . . . Write Box R, *The Times*, E.C.4.'

From this and similar advertisements, it seems that if the private schoolroom is to survive at all, it must be in some communal form; in the way that so many historic country-houses can only survive by becoming hospitals, rest-centres, cultural museums, or, simply by their owners opening their doors to sightseers. What a change of attitude to the one expressed by Miss Hardman in *Shirley* who declared that, 'Governesses must ever be kept in a sort of isolation. It is the only means of maintaining that distance which the reserve of English manners and decorum of English families exact.'

In spite of the overwhelming number of girls who prefer school life to home education, the demand for a good, reliable governess still exists. In fact, Miss Collett, who keeps the Governess Register at the GBI told me, this demand is on the increase, which is interesting. The sad thing is that there are few of the old type of 'vocational' governesses coming forward though professional conditions have improved enormously.

Salaries, for instance, are up to between £150 and £200 and more a year for a private governess. A certain security, too, is assured a governess in her old age; there are many more pensions and special grants available since the days when Charlotte Brontë and her sisters were governesses. In 1847, when *Jane Eyre* was published, the first GBI Home for retired governesses went by the hideous name of 'Asylum for Decayed Governesses'. It was opened at Kentish Town and remained there till 1867. Today, there are the up-to-date and comfortable Queen Mary Homes at Chislehurst and the Ada Lewis Homes at Beckenham where an old governess, past work, can have her own bed-sitting room, furnished with her own things. Having lived her life in other people's houses, it has been found that she is happiest living in this way on retirement.

The English governess has always made herself popular when in service abroad with foreign families, and, generally speaking, is extremely long-lived; perhaps, on account of her spartan habits. This is certainly borne out in the case of Miss Isabella Haynes who has achieved the remarkable age of 102 and is still going strong. She leads an interested and cheerful life in one of the Queen Mary Homes at Chislehurst.

It is sad, I think, to be told at this moment of writing that the 'vocational', old-time governess like Selina Trimmer, as opposed to her modern descendant, who only wishes to do 'a little governessing' in between finding a better job, getting married, or merely collecting some money to see her through college, is such a *rara avis*. For the English governess has been a great civilising agent in the past. She could still be a powerful influence for the good in educating modern girlhood.

As yet there is no substitute for the old-fashioned governess, dedicated to her profession, who brought up many a backward child or gave affection and confidence to the adolescent girl who had lost her mother. In the past, a governess brought into bloom many a rare and sometimes difficult character which today could be, and sometimes is, warped or retarded when one of a crowd in a classroom where small attention is given the problem child.

There is little doubt now that education has been made too easy during the last twenty years. From all sides, the factory, the army and the commercial world, we hear how many boys and girls cannot write – sometimes even read – correctly these days. Lately, there came an announcement from the Council of the Royal College of Nursing that there are young student nurses so ignorant of arithmetic that they cannot safely measure drugs and medicine. There is certainly much to be said, after all, for the old-fashioned governess's simple teaching of The Three Rs. When a governess of ninety-one, now retired, was asked her opinion of education today, she replied: 'My opinion of education is, I am afraid, old-fashioned as I believe in a sound foundation of reading, writing, spelling, and the four rules of arithmetic – and also, if really necessary, corporal punishment. We cannot go wrong if we follow the Bible teaching: "Train up a child in the way it should go, and when he is old, he will not depart from it".'

This is sound advice. At her best, as we have seen, the English governess played a most important rôle in educating men and women destined to shoulder great responsibilities and fulfil great careers. Under her devoted and selfless care, they grew up to obey their parents and all those put in authority over them; to be gentle and courteous in their manner, respecting old age and the rights of the human individual. It is these attributes that survive long after lesson-books have been put away. They are far more important too than having the most-up-to-date teaching methods practised on one in what are called 'advanced' schools.

In conclusion, then, as I gaze regretfully after the vanishing figure of my heroine, whose story I have tried to tell, I should like to repeat Jane Loudon's words that 'the safest, healthiest, the pleasantest and most effectual and cheapest form of Education' may well prove to be still under a good governess.

LONDON 1947   ALTHORNE 1953

SOURCES

ANON *The Private Governess*. The Literary Souvenir, 1826.

ANON *Recollections of a Royal Governess*. Hutchinson, 1915.

ARMITAGE-SMITH, SYDNEY *John Of Gaunt*. Constable, 1904.

ASHDOWN, MARGARET *Elizabeth Elstob, the Learned Saxonist*. The Modern Language Review, vol xx.

ASHTON, HELEN *Parson Austen's Daughter*. Collins, 1949.

AUSTEN, JANE *Mansfield Park*.
Emma.
Letters to her Sister Cassandra, edited by W. R. Chapman, 2 vols. Oxford University Press, 1932.

BALLARD, GEORGE *Memoirs Of The Learned Ladies*. 1725.

BECKENDORFF, COUNT PAUL *Last Days At Tsarskoe Selo*. Heinemann.

BENHAM *Catherine and Crawford Tait: A Memoir*. Macmillan, 1885.

BENNETT, THE REVEREND JOHN *Letters to a Young Lady*. 1795.

BICKNELL, ANNA L. *Life in the Tuileries Under the Second Empire*. T. Fisher Unwin, 1895.

BRONTËS, THE *Lives, Friendships and Correspondence*. Edited by Thomas James Wise and Alexander Symington. 4 vols. Shakespeare Head Press, 1932.

BRONTË, ANNE *Complete Poems*. Edited by Clement K. Shorter. Hodder and Stoughton, 1921.
Agnes Grey.
The Tenant of Wildfell Hall.

BRONTË, CHARLOTTE *Complete Poems*.
The Twelve Adventures and Other Stories. Edited by Clement K. Shorter. Hodder and Stoughton, 1925.
The Professor.

Jane Eyre.

Shirley.

Villette.

Emma, A Fragment.

Biographical Notice, Introductions to Wuthering Heights and Agnes Grey .

BRONTË, EMILY *Complete Poems.* Edited from the MSS by C. W. Hatfield. Columbia University Press and Oxford University Press, 1941.

Wuthering Heights.

Gondal Poems, now published from the MSS in the British Museum. Edited by Helen Brown and Joan Mott. Shakespeare Head Press, 1938.

BROWNE, MARY *The Diary Of a Girl in France in* 1821. John Murray, 1898. Reprinted 1950.

BRUNEL, ROSAMUND GOTCH *Maria, Lady Callcott.* John Murray, 1937.

Letters of Lady Charlotte Bury.

CALDERON DE LA BASCA, MADELEINE *Life in Mexico.* Chapman and Hall, 1863.

Handbook to Chatsworth.

CLARKE, ISABEL *Maria Edgeworth.* Hutchinson, 1950.

CRUSE, AMY *The Englishman and His Books in the Early* 19th *Century.* Harrap, 1930.

CUNNINGTON, C. WILLETT *Feminine Attitudes in the* 19th *Century.* Heinemann, 1935.

DAVIDSON, ANGUS *Edward Lear, A Biography.* John Murray, 1938.

DAVISON, EDITH *Private Papers.* (Unpublished.)

DELAFIELD, E. M. *Ladies and Gentlemen in Victorian Fiction.* The Hogarth Press, 1937.

The Letters of Mrs Delany, vols 2-6. Edited by Lady Llanover. Richard Bentley, 1861.

EAGAR, M. *Six Years at the Russian Court.* Hurst and Blackett, 1906.

EDGEWORTH, RICHARD LOVELL AND MARIA *Practical Education*, 1798.

ELSTOB, ELIZABETH *The English Saxon Homily on the Birthday of St Gregory*, 1709.

FIELD, RACHEL *All This and Heaven Too.*

GARDINER, DOROTHY *English Girlhood at School.* Oxford University Press, 1929.

GASKELL, MRS *The Life of Charlotte Brontë.* Smith and Elder, 1870.
Wives and Daughters.

GLYNN, GRYLLS R. *Claire Clairmont.* John Murray, 1939.

GOSSE, EDMUND *Father and Son.* Heinemann, 1907.

GRAHAM, MARIA *Journal of a Residence in Chile.* Longmans, 1824.
Journal of a Voyage to Brazil. John Murray, 1824.
Private Journal. (Unpublished.)

GRANT, ELIZABETH *Memoirs of a Highland Lady.* John Murray, 1898. Reprinted 1950.

HAM, ELIZABETH *By Herself.* Faber, 1945.

HAMILTON, MRS MARY *Green and Gold.* Allen Wingate, 1948.

HARDING, BERTITA *Amazonian Throne.* Harrap, 1940.

The Heber Letters, 1762–1832. The Batchworth Press, 1950.

HEWLETT, MAURICE *Wiltshire Essays.* Humphrey Milford, 1921.

HITCHENS, ROBERT *The Green Carnation.* 1894.

HOLE, CHRISTINA *Family Life.* Batsford, 1948.

The Girlhood of Maria Josepha Holroyd. Edited by Jane Adeane. Green and Co., 1897.

The Essays of Mrs Jameson. Richard Bentley, 1860.

KIRKE, THE REVEREND JOHN *The Mother of the Wesleys.* 1876.

KNIGHT, CHARLES *The Governess.* 1844.

KYLE, ELIZABETH *The Skater's Waltz.* Peter Davies, 1944.
The Lady's Companion, vol I.

LANDON, MARGARET *Anna Leonowens and the King of Siam.* Harrap, 1945.

LANG, MRS ANDREW *Men, Women and Minxes.* Longmans, Green and Co., 1912.

LAVERTY, MAURA *None so Human.* Cape, 1944.

LEONOWENS, ANNA *Siamese Harem Life.* Arthur Barker, 1952.

LEVESON GOWER, LORD GRANVILLE *Private Correspondence.* 1761–1821. Edited by Castalia, Countess Granville, John Murray, 1916.

LEVESON GOWER, IRIS *The Face Without a Frown.* Frederick Muller, 1944.

LINDSAY, LORD *The Lives of the Lindsays.* John Murray, 1849.

LOTT, EMMELINE *The English Governess in Egypt and Turkey.* Richard Bentley, 1866.
Nights in The Harem. Chapman and Hall, 1867.

MACLEAN, FITZROY *Eastern Approaches.* Cape, 1948.

MASSON, MADELINE *Lady Anne Barnard.* George Unwin, 1946.

MITFORD, NANCY (Editor) *The Ladies of Alderley.* Chapman and Hall.

MORGAN, LADY SYDNEY *O'Donnell.*

OCAMPO, VICTORIA *Testimonios* (Segunda Series). Sur, 1941.

ORIGO, IRIS *Allegra.* The Hogarth Press, 1935.

PERCIVAL, ALICE *The English Miss.* Harrap, 1939.

PHILLIPS, M., AND TOMKINSON, W.S. *English Women in Life and Letters.* Oxford University Press, 1922.

RAY, GORDON N. *New Light on Thackeray.*

RICHARDSON, SAMUEL *Clarissa Harlow,* 1750.

SCOTT, WALTER *The Bluestocking Ladies.* John Green, 1947.
Letters from Members of Sir Walter Scott's Family. Grant Richards, 1905.

SCOTT THOMPSON, GLADYS *Mrs Arthur Strong: A Memoir.* Cohen and West, 1949.

The Russells in Bloomsbury. Cape, 1940.

SHENSTONE, WILLIAM *The Schoolmistress.* 1764.

SHORTER, CLEMENT K. *Charlotte Brontë and Her Circle.* Hodder and Stoughton, 1896.

Family Papers of the Stewart Brownes of Tallentire. (Unpublished.)

STUART, D. M. *Men and Women of Plantaganet England.* Harrap, 1932.

THACKERAY, WILLIAM *Vanity Fair.*

Letters.

TREVELYAN, G. M. *Illustrated Social History.* Longmans, Green and Co., 1949.

Letters of Selina Trimmer, 1786–1829. Chatsworth MSS.

WALLAS, ADA *Before the Bluestockings.* Allen and Unwin, 1929.

WATT, MARGARET *The Parson's Wife.* Faber, 1943.

WEETON, MISS *Journal of A Governess.* 2 vols. Oxford University Press, 1937.

WEIGALL, R. *An Elizabethan Gentlewoman.* Quarterly Review, 1911.

WOOD, MRS HENRY *The Channings,* 1862.

WOODHAM SMITH, CECIL *Florence Nightingale.* Constable, 1950.

WOOLF, VIRGINIA *The Common Reader.* Hogarth Press, 1925.

YONGE, CHARLOTTE *Hopes and Fears.*

Womankind. Mozley and Smith, 1876.

YOUNG, G.M. *Victorian England.* Oxford University Press, 1936.